Igni[illegible]
Sales Strategy

A Field Guide to Accelerating your Pipeline

ignite selling
Sales Simulations that Inspire®

Steve Gielda
Kevin Jones

First paperback edition February 2022

ISBN 979-888680993-0 (paperback)

www.Igniteselling.com

Acknowledgements

Writing this book was something we were looking forward to for the past few years. When we published our first book in 2012, *Premeditated Selling: Tools for Developing the Right Strategy for Every Opportunity*, we were in early stages of developing the tools that the strategic toolkit we call our Ignite Your Strategy Snapshot tools. We are grateful for the customers, marketing partners, and friends that helped bring this second book to life.

Though this book was a lot of fun to write, it was hard work and required a lot of research into our customers' win/loss analysis data, many interviews with several top-performing salespeople and managers, and the assessment of the key business metrics our clients achieved because of implementing our strategic snapshot tools. We would like to offer a special thanks to our publishing and marketing team at BME, especially Gabe Arnold and Wally Winiefredo for their guidance and patience throughout the writing process. We'd also like to thank Emma Carter for her graphic design support. In addition, a big thank you to our friends and client partners; Alain Adam, Meredith Bon Tempo, Steve Milton, David Austin, Jon Gingrich, Shane Robinson, Kevin King, John Lee, Mike Wijas, John Hoskins and so many others that gave of their time to provide us the insights and support we needed to complete this endeavor.

Of course, we couldn't and wouldn't have done this without the blessings and support of our family. We want to offer up a sincere thank you to Sherry (Steve's wife) and Donna (Kevin's wife) for giving us the gift of encouragement and support to focus on this project that we know took valuable time away from the family. We'd also like to thank Steve's family; Kayla Miranda, son-in-law Bruno Miranda and his grandson Kaden Miranda, as well as Kevin's family Aidan and Poppy. These individuals are one of the primary reasons we work so hard.

TABLE OF CONTENTS

Our selling organization has deployed and utilized most of the off the shelf sales methodologies, but Ignite your Sales Strategy has a custom approach with simple tools that allows for a consistent, easy to adopt selling approach for all our unique business units.

John Lee
Director Global Sales Training, Urology & Pelvic Health
Boston Scientific

CHAPTER 1

Thinking and Acting Strategically

This book is a project we originally conceived as a way to codify and disseminate many of the client assessments, win/loss analyses and best practices we've observed over the years. It is our hope that it helps salespeople better analyze opportunities and develop strategic opportunity plans to help accelerate your pipeline revenue, beat out the competition and win more business.

As sales leaders ourselves, we know how books like this get used. Some folks embrace these ideas in whole or in part and begin implementing them straight away. Ironically, this book is not really meant for them; they are top performers because they are already doing much of what we describe. Other salespeople may read this book but choose to disregard the ideas completely, despite the fact that those are the people who typically have the most to gain from implementing these "success ideas."

However, it is neither the top performer nor the low performer who we had in mind when we conceived this book. It's the lot in the middle we wrote it for, the salespeople who hit their numbers but still have room to grow. They win some and lose some, like most salespeople, but they ought to be winning more than they are losing.

This book will help show you how to develop a sales strategy for each unique opportunity inside your accounts. In this book, we're providing you with a set of simple yet impactful tools that are proven to help improve your strategic thinking and strategic planning. We'll encourage you to challenge the assumptions you might make while working on a key sales opportunity.

We've also compiled a shortlist of Strategic Validation Questions at the end of each chapter to assist with your planning process.

Let's Meet the Stars of Our Show

To begin, let's introduce you to our friends Mike and Susan.

Susan and Mike work at a global high-end technology firm with over 750 salespeople worldwide, selling capital equipment, software, technical support and professional services.

Susan is what we'd describe as a **top-performing salesperson,** winning President's Club consistently over the past 5 years. She stayed in the top 10 percent of salespeople since she started with the company and even turned down the opportunity to be promoted to sales manager.

She displays great organizational skills, is a strategic thinker and proactively seeks out the feedback and opinions from others she respects.

Part of how Susan has achieved top-performing sales has to do with how she adapts to and utilizes the six-stage pipeline process we developed for the company both she and Mike work for. She consistently follows the critical milestones and tasks for each phase of the sales process. In addition, Susan leverages the tools she has been provided to challenge her strategic thinking and opportunity planning.

Mike, on the other hand, has worked for this company for over 8 years, excelling at building relationships with his existing customers. He is considered successful by most of his peers, and any manager would've been lucky to have him on their team. But as much as we like Mike, he's still what we'd call an **average performer**, hitting his targets in some months, while missing them in others.

While Mike is organized and a hard worker, he often relies on discounts to win sales and isn't one to spend a great deal of time putting together strategic plans for his sales opportunities. He occasionally hits his quota and has only reached the President's Club twice in the past 8 years.

Now, we're introducing you to our friends for a reason. After working with both of them through their company for a while, we've noticed that their experiences truly help illustrate how the tools we provide can help *you* win more and lose less. We'll use their experiences throughout the book to show you how you can utilize our tools to challenge your critical thinking skills and become a top-performing salesperson.

So, without further ado, let's get into our first story about Mike!

On one summer day, Mike lost a sale that was so big he could have hit a third of his yearly quota with it.

From a tactical standpoint, Mike felt fully prepared for the sales meeting because this time, he'd done his homework. He made the calls, gathered some critical insights, planned the questions he wanted to ask and he knew exactly how he was going to open the conversation with the senior-level buyer. He even thought about potential objections to his solution and knew how he would overcome them.

The meeting went almost exactly as Mike had planned, so he left feeling confident that he was in an excellent position to win the business. Unfortunately, less than 24 hours after his meeting had concluded, Mike got a call from the customer letting him know they had decided to sign the contract with his competitor.

Mike felt like the rug had been pulled out from under him.

To Mike, the opportunity had seemed a sure thing. A sure thing that was now dead. But why? A mental post-mortem of any sales opportunity is—or ought to be—standard for all salespeople. Especially for an opportunity that slid inexplicably from the "won" to the "lost" column.

If you're like Mike, questions of what could have been will haunt your thoughts after having lost a sale. What did you miss? Did you understand the client's decision criteria? Who was the competition speaking with inside the account that you weren't? Was your competitor's solution really better than yours? At the time, Mike had all these same questions.

Ultimately, despite his homework, Mike learned that **he had failed to use his company's sales pipeline effectively**, overlooking key steps. The key milestone in the pipeline that could have prevented him from losing the sale was simple: he failed to understand the decision criteria the customer was using to compare Mike's solution to the competition.

Mike should have uncovered the customer's decision criteria *before* he went on his visit to speak with the customer. Then, armed with that information, he could have had better insights into how his customer intended to make this important and expensive decision and positioned his solution more effectively.

Mike, like most average performers, has a good understanding of foundational selling skills. Additionally, he frequently puts in the time to develop pre-meeting plans, opening statements, pre-planned questions and ideas on how to overcome anticipated objections. These are the foundational things many salespeople do to prepare for a sales meeting.

However, top performers, like Susan, do more than just the fundamentals to secure a win. In these next chapters, we will explore what makes top performers different from average performers when it comes to using process and strategic planning tools to win key sales opportunities. Ultimately, our aim is to help you be less like Mike so you can win more and lose less.

You Can Lead a Horse to Water...

We wish we could tell you that every salesperson we've ever trained on the sales pipeline process or strategy development has embraced the ideas we've taught and successfully and vigorously implemented these tools into their day-to-day activities.

But developing a strategy or following a well-defined sales process sounds akin to planning, which many salespeople simply equate to paperwork, and we don't know many salespeople who even remotely like paperwork. Filling out forms and reports can feel like a waste of time; and indeed, it does keep sellers from really crucial sales activities, like actually talking to customers.

Even top performers like Susan can be skeptical of the impact a well-defined sales pipeline process and strategy tools will bring them. In fact, after we launched the sales pipeline process and a series of simple strategy tools designed to help build proactive strategies for Susan's company, we encountered resistance from Susan.

Now, remember, Susan is ranked as one of the top salespeople in her company year after year. Although she told me she was grateful for the support we had provided her company, she didn't believe she needed to use the new pipeline process or the strategy tools because she already felt that she naturally does this type of analysis in her head.

So, naturally, I wanted to challenge her thinking. On the back of a napkin, I drew out one of our strategy tools, called the Influencer Snapshot®, and I asked her to help me populate the model. It took less than 60 seconds, and I complimented her knowledge of understanding the key influencers inside the account.

Then I asked her three more questions:

1) How do you know this picture is accurate? In other words, who have you validated this picture with inside the account?

She responded, "No one."

Then I asked her my second question; 2) Who is your competition speaking to inside this account that you're not?

She responded slower this time. "I'm not sure."

That brought me to my third question; 3) What's at risk if you don't know the answers to these questions?

That got her to understand very quickly that sometimes just drawing the picture and having someone else look at it with you can help bring the picture of a sale into better focus.

Our aim is to help you *think differently about strategic opportunity planning*. We believe that all sales strategic planning efforts should be easy to use and have immediate relevance.

With this in mind, we have designed a set of tools we call Strategic Snapshots.

The Strategic Snapshot tools are designed to help you evaluate a sales opportunity from various angles, providing you insight into your situation, and helping you create proactive strategies for moving the opportunity forward in your sales pipeline.

It's important to keep in mind that every Strategic Snapshot tool doesn't need to be used with every opportunity.

Each of the tools assists you in analyzing opportunities and gathering the information you need to make your next move. Because these are individual tools, you can choose to use the tool you believe is most important at the time. It's rare for a salesperson to use every tool in every strategic planning session.

Because these tools work independently of each other, it's easy for top-performing salespeople to share one or more of the tools with their colleagues in order to gain their perspective on the situation.

We refer to these strategic planning tools as snapshots because they provide a visual "snapshot" or picture in time of what the current situation is for the sales opportunity. As you learn more about the Strategic Snapshot tools, we believe you'll discover that while there isn't always the time or need to develop an in-depth sales strategy for every opportunity, there are definitely accounts that are more complex that require planning.

These are the ideal opportunities where you should take time to stop and think about what should be done differently to secure a win. Sometimes you just need to slow down in order to speed up.

Our Snapshot tools provide a **framework for consistency so that strategic opportunity sales planning is repeatable, and so information can be shared across an enterprise in a commonly understood way**.

A well-designed tool can enable you to evaluate a situation and organize your information. However, it's what you do with the information that matters. As you complete these Snapshot tools, you may identify gaps in your knowledge about your opportunities, which are then up to you to fill to reach the sale.

The "intentional" approach to selling that we present in this book won't win you every opportunity that comes your way, but it will help you win more of them. And if you lose, you will be equipped with the tools to uncover the real reasons why you lost—key information that can empower you to win the next one around.

One important factor to keep in mind when it comes to thinking about the value of our Strategic Snapshot tools is that we consider these tools Strategic ***Opportunity*** Planning tools. The keyword here is ***opportunity***.

Most strategic planning tools are focused on the "Account Plan." Although it's important to have an overall account plan, it is critical to keep in mind there could be multiple, significant opportunities within a single account, all of which could benefit from the clearer picture you will get through the application of these Snapshot tools.

Effectively using the four Strategic Snapshot tools we're providing you will help you find a way to bring complex, potentially difficult and unclear situations into focus.

The four Strategic Snapshot tools are:

1. ***Situational Snapshot®*** - a tool to help you better understand the buying factors impacting the opportunity.
2. ***Influencer Snapshot®*** - a tool to help you better leverage the key influencers involved in the decision.
3. ***Competitive Snapshot®*** - a tool to help you identify and influence your customer's decision criteria.
4. ***Value Snapshot®*** - a tool to help you better align the value of your solutions to the goals and metrics that matter most to the customer.

Situational Snapshot® - Assessing the Buying Factors

The Situational Snapshot® is a tool **to assist in assessing the key buying factors that impact complex sales opportunities.** By understanding certain factors, such as urgency, decision timelines and a customer's purchasing process, you can alter your sales strategy to enhance your resources and strengths.

For instance, had Mike understood the buying factors impacting his sales opportunity, he could have anticipated the need to alter his approach and then explored ways to provide solutions his competitors couldn't.

We'll explore this topic and tool a bit further in Chapter 3. We'll challenge you to think about the answers to questions like: What is the buying process going to be for this specific purchase? How long is the customer going to take to make a decision? What is the sense of urgency driving your customer's buying process today? Is there a need for consensus among the decision-makers or is there a diversity of opinion?

In today's market, we must be able to answer these questions plus many others regarding our customers' buying factors.

Influencer Snapshot® - Leveraging the Key Influencer

The Influencer Snapshot® is a tool **to assist in the analysis of the individuals involved in the customer decision process—their influence in the decision and their perceptions of potential solution providers.** By gaining insight into your advocates and adversaries, including who they support and why, you can develop a plan of action to capitalize on your positive relationships while minimizing potential threats.

Just as Mike learned, the key influencers aren't just the head of the department. In complex sales, there are often multiple key influencers, many of which might not seem obvious. If Mike had asked a few more questions about the role, influence and perception of others, he might not have ended up being surprised. If you don't know who your competition is speaking to, then you're likely putting your opportunity to win the business at risk.

In Chapter 4, we're going to take a deeper dive into this topic and provide you with the Influencer Snapshot® tool, which will help you **better analyze the key influencers in every sales opportunity**.

We'll challenge you to think about the answers to questions such as: What's been said or done to make you believe your advocate is really your advocate? Is there a way to leverage your advocates to neutralize your adversaries? If so, how can that be done? Who are your competitors' advocates? What are you doing to win them over?

We'll help you better analyze all the key influencers involved in your opportunity so you can develop a smart strategy to leverage advocate support.

Competitive Snapshot® - Identifying and Influencing the Customer's Decision Criteria

The Competitive Snapshot® is a tool **to assist in organizing the customer's decision criteria in order to boost your solution's strengths and minimize its weaknesses.**

Identifying and influencing the customer's decision criteria is one of the most often ignored elements of strategic planning. We conducted a large number of post-mortems for lost sales.

In these post-mortems, we've asked the salesperson: "Why do you think you lost this opportunity?" The most common culprit (in 88 percent of the responses) where salespeople place the blame for a lost sale is "Price." The salespeople we've surveyed constantly tell us the competitor won the deal because they provided a lower price.

When we ask our follow-up question, "What other two or three decision criteria did the customer use to make this decision?", we hear crickets. It's absolutely silent! The salespeople we've interviewed don't know any decision criteria other than price. It's no wonder price is the number one reason they believe they lost.

By thinking broadly about the criteria a customer will use to make a decision and knowing your strengths and weaknesses against those criteria, you can develop a strategy to capitalize on your strengths and minimize your weaknesses.

In Chapter 5, we're going to challenge you to **reassess your understanding of your customer's decision criteria**. You'll be prompted to consider questions such as: What decision criteria does the customer believe is your strongest asset? Who have you spoken with to confirm the customer's decision criteria? If there are multiple decision-makers, do they all agree on the same decision criteria? Whose decision criteria matter the most and why? How does the customer perceive your ability to meet their decision criteria?

Value Snapshot® - Aligning the Value of Your Solution to the Goals and Metrics that Matter Most to the Customer

The Value Snapshot® is a tool that **assists in aligning the value of your solution to the goals and metrics that matter most to the customer**. Effectively understanding how the customer will measure success enables a salesperson to more effectively position his/her solution.

Salespeople have been taught for years that they can win by understanding customer needs and by effectively demonstrating how their solution can address those needs. Unfortunately, evidence suggests there is more to sales than just understanding a customer's needs. In Chapter 6, we're going to stretch your thinking around how a salesperson truly creates Value.

This will require you to have a firm grasp on the business metrics your client is striving to improve and then align how your solution specifically helps improve those metrics. Going back to Mike's lost sale, if he had a better understanding of the business metrics his customer was striving to improve and was able to effectively quantify the value of his solution in his first meeting, he might have won the sale.

In Chapter 6, we're going to push you to think about: What are the most important business outcomes your customer will receive by implementing your solution? How will your customer measure your solution's value? What metrics have you chosen to measure the value impact of the outcomes? What detracts from the measurable value of your solution?

All too frequently salespeople underestimate the importance of quantifying the value of their solution. They assume the customer can make the connection between their solution and the impact it can have on the customer's business metrics. Unfortunately, these kinds of assumptions can make the difference between winning or losing the opportunity.

Chapter 1 Summary

In this chapter, we previewed our Ignite Selling Snapshot® tools helping you understand that sometimes leveraging a simple tool that challenges your strategic thinking and common assumptions, but makes the difference between winning or losing. In addition, we introduced you to the two main characters, Mike and Susan, who will help us throughout this book to understand how to win more and lose less.

Our Snapshot® tools:

- ***Situational Snapshot®***, Chapter 3 - a tool to help you better understand the buying factors impacting the opportunity.
- ***Influencer Snapshot®***, Chapter 4 - a tool to help you better leverage the key influencers involved in the decision.
- ***Competitive Snapshot®***, Chapter 5 - a tool to help you identify and influence your customer's decision criteria.
- ***Value Snapshot®***, Chapter 6 - a tool that will help you better align solutions to the goals and metrics that matter most to the customer.

Understanding your organization's sales process and the milestones that define each stage is the lifeblood of the commercial team and the foundation for all other cross-functional activity. ***Ignite Your Sales Strategy*** *is proven and will serve the needs of any sales organization in search of increasing revenue!*

Cory Sinning
AVP Sales
Intersect ENT, Inc

Chapter 2

Building a Sales Pipeline

A Recipe for Success

We are big fans of good food. In our opinion, one of the best places in the world to get great food is New Orleans, Louisiana. So many great chefs and restaurants come from the New Orleans area that it's hard to keep count, and while we are no Emeril Legasse, we do like to try our hands at cooking a few complicated New Orleans-style recipes from time to time.

Any good recipe, regardless of how simple or complicated it may be, creates successful, repeatable and measurable results. While it might be okay to deviate from a recipe from time to time, when you skip steps or change the order of the steps, it can have a dramatic impact on the outcome.

A "well-defined sales pipeline" is like a salesperson's "recipe for success." If it is built right, the sales pipeline will consist of clearly defined steps – what we call **critical milestones.** A ***critical milestone is a strategic action that if not taken, could put the opportunity at risk***. These critical milestones serve as the steps in the company's recipe for sales success. Top performers use their company's well-defined sales process and the milestones that comprise it just as they would the directions of a recipe: *"For best and repeatable results, follow the steps in the order they have been provided to you. Skip steps at your own risk!"*

But how does a company come up with a well-defined sales process? How do you build a recipe for sales success? If we wanted to come up with the perfect recipe for gumbo, we would pull together a group of chefs from the top restaurants in New Orleans. Although each of these chefs may have a unique way of making gumbo, there would likely be some commonalities in their approach, the steps they would take and the necessary ingredients. We could combine their knowledge and opinions to build a recipe that could become the standard that others could follow to get a consistent and outstanding result.

Creating the Recipe

We saw this story play out when we were working with Mike and Susan's company. The VP of sales was striving significantly to improve the team's forecasting. Like many organizations, forecasting was about as accurate as guessing when a double zero would come up on the roulette table.

Salespeople didn't have an effective or consistent way to predict when their opportunities would close. Each region had its own way of doing things. This caused many problems for the team, and of course for the company itself.

The biggest concern was providing a more accurate sales forecast to the Chief Revenue Officer each quarter. If projections were off by more than 5 percent in either direction, the VP of sales had to explain why and justify it, a verbal shuffle that resembled a rhetorical Riverdance.

The VP wanted to build a more rigorous sales pipeline process, complete with detailed key milestones so the team could get a more accurate sales forecast. In addition, they could also reduce the likelihood of opportunities stalling in the pipeline and get the added benefit of a more strategically minded sales team.

We were asked to help develop a new sales pipeline process that would consistently meet the demand to provide accurate forecasts to the board. We knew that we had to gather the top performers from the company and identify the critical milestones that would provide a proven and repeatable recipe for success. In addition, we knew we had to provide a set of simple, easy-to-use tools to help the sales team effectively execute and achieve the critical milestones.

So, we began the project with data collection. We interviewed the top-performing regional sales directors, sales managers and account managers across the customer-facing enterprise. (It is important to note that neither Mike nor Susan were included in our data collection.) We wanted to learn three things.

First, we had a hunch that those top performers did a better job than the rest of the salespeople in truly understanding how a customer was making their buying decision. What we wanted to know was what those top performers were doing to have clarity around their customer's decision process, and how they would define their customer's decision process.

Second, we wanted to know what critical actions these top performers were taking in the early, middle and late stages of their sales process. We wanted to use this information to define the critical milestones in each stage of their new sales pipeline process. In addition, we wanted to understand: what sort of ground rules were they using to move customers out of one stage and into another?

Third, we wanted to know what managers were doing to be a value-adding resource to their sales team throughout the process. Did the manager merely inspect what they expected by asking questions to test the understanding of what the salesperson knew or didn't know? Or, were the managers challenging the critical thinking and common assumptions the salesperson might have been making to help develop alternative strategies to accelerate the customers decision process?

Remember, when we initially started working with Mike and Susan's company, they didn't have a well-defined and centrally controlled sales pipeline process across the enterprise. Some regions did it one way, some did it another. But among the top performers, there emerged a consistent theme: the top performers utilized a consistent and rigorous process for their region. Whether it involved six pipeline stages, or three or four or 10, and they communicated frequently about opportunities' progress—or lack thereof—through the pipeline's stages.

The unfortunate reality, though, was that the top performers were not any more successful at forecasting than average or below-average performers were.

This was not acceptable to the company. So, working in collaboration with a cross-functional team, we designed and implemented a rigorous, workable six-stage sales pipeline. The six stages were:

Stage 1 - Opportunity Qualification
Stage 2 - Needs Development
Stage 3 - Solution Identification
Stage 4 - Implementation Resolution
Stage 5 - Contract Confirmation
Stage 6 - Implementation & Adoption

To be honest, the VP of sales was not originally impressed with the six stages.

He actually said, "Seriously? I paid you guys how much and this is what you deliver? I could have found this online with a simple Google search." We did not blame him for his first reaction (there is something wonderful about a client who speaks their mind). And, in one significant way, he was right!

The names of our six stages were not delivered on stone tablets from Sinai. They were not particularly innovative. They were just six stages, with no magic attached to the number six.

What *did* impress the VP of Sales—what made this approach different from some of the company's flavor-of-the-week approaches from their past—was the unambiguous way in which the six stages were delineated, and the key milestones and metrics built into each stage.

Agreeing upon the number of stages in your sales pipeline—and naming them in a way that is both memorable and denotative—is indeed a good idea, but it is only a single step. More important than fixating on the right number of stages is clearly defining each of them in a way that drives the sales team to ***think and act*** in a more strategic and proactive manner.

What constitutes the first stage? What are the critical milestones that must be accomplished? How does a salesperson validate for themselves that they have effectively accomplished the critical milestones? And how is it distinct from the second stage? What milestones have to be met to move an opportunity from Stage 3 to Stage 4? What strategic actions have to take place?

These criteria—the activities and milestones—ought to reflect the day-to-day selling life of the customer-facing enterprise. **Remember, we define a**

milestone as a critical sales activity that, if NOT done, puts the opportunity at risk.

Is identifying the critical business metrics the customer is striving to improve next year a critical sales activity? If so, it ought to be a milestone ("Identified top three critical metrics of the customer") in one of the stages. Is developing a strategy to neutralize any potential adversaries important to your team? Then this ought to be a critical milestone in one of the earlier stages of the sales pipeline. (By the way, the completion of an Influencer Snapshot® could be a useful tool to help accomplish this particular milestone.)

Establishing the critical milestones for each stage makes it easier for salespeople and managers to communicate with clarity where they are in the sales pipeline process.

For example, if one salesperson tells another that Acme Biotech is in Stage 3 of the sales pipeline, the second salesperson knows that each of the milestones in Stages 1 and 2 has been met. With a bit of Q&A between them, the second salesperson knows **what milestones have been completed properly and which milestones have not**. To move Acme Biotech to Stage 4, the salesperson has to simply accomplish the critical milestones in Stage 3. This will probably also give everyone involved an idea of what needs to happen to close this opportunity and by when.

So, coupled closely with naming and defining each stage is ensuring that the pipeline process itself is integrated with the day-to-day sales activities. That is, selling activities should fit with the pipeline.

Here's an example of a sales pipeline process we designed for this client:

Stage 1 Opportunity Qualification	Stage 2 Needs Development	Stage 3 Solution Identification	Stage 4 Demonstrating Capabilities	Stage 5 Contract Confirmation	Stage 6 Driving Adoption
•All key influencers in the decision process identified •Identified the advocates and adversaries around making a change •Gained clear understanding of the business metrics the company is striving to improve •Understand the customer's decision process	•Needs and downside risks of not changing identified •Identified the customers compelling reason to act •Developed strategy to neutralize adversaries •Confirmed availability of budget	•Buyers understand link between our solutions and their needs •Customer decision criteria identified •Quantified the value of our solution with top key influencers •Go/No Go decision discussed with customer	•Demonstrated how our solution better aligns to the customers key decision criteria •Validated our adversaries are neutralized •Confirmed key influencers are aligned to implementing our solution •Implementation risk identified and resolved	•Contract submitted to client for authorization •Legal review conducted. Concerns resolved •Confirmed delivery processes are established •Training is scheduled for new users	•Conducted training on new systems •Established plan to leverage our key advocates •Conducted first 90 Day business review •Promoted success of new system through organization and peers

Once our team of leaders agreed upon the steps and critical milestones, we had essentially "version one" of this company's "recipe for success." The next step was to educate the sales team, update the company's CRM and reporting tools with the stages and milestones, and prepare the managers to coach the new sales pipeline process. Once implemented, this pipeline process had **five distinct advantages** for Susan and Mike's company:

First Advantage

Salespeople are clear about what they need to accomplish to keep the customer's decision process moving forward. Too often average performers walk in and out of their customers' offices without doing anything strategic to help drive the customer closer to a decision.

With clear milestones in each stage of the sales pipeline process, Susan, Mike and the rest of the sales team could assess which milestones had not been achieved for that stage, and then develop smart call plans to achieve those objectives.

For example, if a salesperson has an opportunity in Stage 3, and one of the incomplete milestones is to validate the customer's decision criteria, then the call objective is clear.

Second Advantage

It accelerates the sales cycle. Top salespeople are proactively driving opportunities through the sales pipeline, versus playing a passive or reactive role. Having smart and clear milestones at each stage fosters momentum-building activities because salespeople are motivated to get the customers to take action.

Our research has proven that when salespeople are held accountable for accomplishing the critical milestones in each stage, they are able to accelerate the pipeline process by 37 percent. This means they are closing more business faster.

Third Advantage

The salesperson and their managers have absolute clarity about where the opportunity is in the pipeline. An opportunity cannot move into Stage 3 until it has met all the critical milestones for Stage 1 and Stage 2. And a salesperson cannot promote an opportunity to an advanced stage before its time, so nobody gets false optimism about a deal's likelihood to close.

Fourth Advantage

Sales managers can now quickly identify where a salesperson may need help. Sales managers often spend hours conducting "account reviews" with their teams without having any clear objectives for the conversation.

Our research has shown that over 55 percent of opportunities "stall" in the middle to late stages of the pipeline process, and what's more shocking is that over 80 percent of the salespeople we interviewed blame the customer as to why the opportunity has stalled. Establishing critical milestones for each stage of the sales pipeline process allows the manager to quickly identify which accounts seem to be "stuck" in the pipeline. They can collaborate with their salespeople on developing action plans to get the opportunity "unstuck" and begin moving towards the finish line.

Without milestones in each stage of the pipeline, managers may conduct account reviews with good intentions, but they can't establish which direction the seller should move to secure the business opportunity.

Fifth Advantage

Establishing clear milestones in each stage of the pipeline process creates a set of forecast metrics that senior sales leaders can rely on. If the senior sales leaders can get their entire team working towards achieving the key milestones throughout the pipeline process, they will be more able to establish accurate forecasts that allow the operations, manufacturing and finance departments to make better business decisions for the company. Our research has shown that when managers hold their teams accountable for accomplishing the milestones in each stage, sales forecasting can be improved by 65 percent.

The sales pipeline model we designed for Susan's and Mike's sales team quickly improved the company's forecasting accuracy, to say nothing of the sales team's increased interest in living the process. Susan and her sales manager became more attuned to warning signs of an opportunity stalling or slowing and worked together proactively to avoid the common pitfalls.

Conversely, they were able to respond more appropriately when an opportunity's forward momentum decreased (because they saw it coming). Over time, the management team established reliable metrics that gave them insights into their business. For instance, they learned that opportunities that entered Stage 3 had a 78 percent chance of closing.

When the opportunity moved into Stage 4, the percentage jumped to 86 percent. The VP of Sales was able to provide the Chief Revenue Officer and other stakeholders, like the manufacturing and finance departments, the accurate forecast they were demanding. More importantly, the salespeople and sales managers had a consistent pipeline process, one that was linked to their day-to-day selling activities.

Keep it Simple

For those who know us, you know that we have a certain affinity for bourbon, and specifically bourbon-based cocktails. I had the opportunity to visit Bardstown, Kentucky with my wife one summer while my daughters were away at summer camp. On our visit, we stopped at the Bardstown Bourbon Company for a cocktail-making class. Now, I have been to my share of cocktail bars and have tried many drinks where I can't even pronounce half of the ingredients. Since I am adventurous, I will try these complicated cocktails. However, the best cocktail I've ever had was the Old Fashioned I made for myself in that cocktail-making class in Bardstown.

And the recipe was so simple:

- 2 dashes of Angostura bitters
- ¼ oz of demerara simple syrup (2:1 sugar-to-water ratio)
- 2 oz .of bourbon.
- Shake with ice – pour into a glass and serve with an orange peel
- Three ingredients. How simple can you get?

We know the details behind a well-defined sales pipeline process are more complicated than my simple Old Fashioned cocktail recipe, but many companies seem intent on developing a sales pipeline process that is so detailed and comprehensive that nobody can read it, much less follow it. It seems that in the corporate world, simplicity is often a bad sign. If it's simple, it must not be complete. If it can be explained by mere mortals instead of MIT honor students or those who are part of Mensa, it's probably not good enough.

This explains the VP of Sales response to our simple six-stage pipeline model. But it's important to remember that simplicity is crucial with processes that need to be scaled across large enterprises.

An effective pipeline process needs to combine simplicity with effectiveness; it not only must be easy to learn and apply across a population of users, but it must also be robust enough to stand up to day-to-day sales rigors. As we've discussed, the challenge is in thoroughly defining each stage, delineating them from one another and clearly distinguishing their boundaries.

To help establish these boundaries, it is important to determine which milestones come before other milestones. When I learned how to make my simple Old Fashioned cocktail, I wondered if it mattered in which order I added my ingredients. It turns out, the answer is yes.

First, always add the cheapest ingredients first in case you make a mistake and have to throw it away. And second, don't add the ice until you are ready to shake it up! In a sales pipeline process, it might be best to understand

and quantify the customer's needs before providing the customer pricing information. The building of your well-defined sales process should help your sales team understand "What comes before what."

I Wanted to Be a Weather Forecaster, But I Couldn't See Any Future In It!

This scene is an all-too-recognizable one. A sales manager somewhere is talking about a pipeline with one of her salespeople. It's a conversation that takes place at least monthly and has the eerie familiarity of déjà vu to salespeople. It might go something like this:

Salesperson: *Yes, I believe we'll close the KNG deal by the end of the month for $250,000, as well as MRG for an additional $125,000.*

Manager: *C'mon. You've been forecasting KNG to close for six months. I'll believe it when I see it!*

You could insert almost any customer, set the story in almost any industry, with any salesperson and manager, and the conversation would still be essentially the same. Senior sales leaders and shareholders want accurate forecasts. Management wants accurate forecasts. And salespeople usually do their best to supply them.

We know many of you are thinking that the only purpose of the sales pipeline process is so that senior sales leaders can keep track of who's working and who's not. More than one salesperson has expressed sentiments similar to this IT client manager: "Forecasting has no value to me as a salesperson. My manager just wants it so he has something to hold over my head until the end of the month."

We suspect that this is truer than managers may care to admit. Yet the reason for this is that bad information from bad sales pipeline management processes yields forecasts that have little value for anyone, except as an enforcement tool. However, **there is tremendous value in managing your customer opportunities in an active sales pipeline management process**.

By following a sales pipeline, you will be able to predict which opportunities you will win or lose, and when a deal might actually close. This predictability helps you ensure the sales forecast is being met, and that you can provide resources for a successful implementation.

Emerging customer relationship management (CRM) software, such as SalesForce.com, Microsoft Dynamics, ZoHo and others, have made great strides in simplifying the reporting process. This ought to have led to better forecasts and improved pipeline management. Yet the problems have persistently survived, and salespeople and managers still have challenges getting the results everyone wants.

The obstacle stems from this simple truth: Good technology layered over processes that do not work yields unsatisfactory results. Too often companies implement a sales pipeline process into their organization to match their shiny new CRMs, without any regard to the core strategic sales activities that salespeople should complete throughout the entire process.

From every sector, in company after company, from seller to seller, we see this same problem occurring with inaccurate sales forecasting. We've found some very simple reasons why forecasts aren't always reliable.

Over-Optimism

Misguided optimism is often to blame for poor sales forecasting.

Most salespeople have a deep reservoir of optimism in their bodies. It's what sustains them in the face of constant rejection. It's what helps them overcome obstacles. It's what allows them to take the lemon they have just been handed and open up a thriving lemonade stand.

This constant optimism so frequently found in salespeople reminds us of the old joke about the dad who wants to teach his optimistic son that life is not always a bowl of cherries or a bed of roses. So instead of presents under his Christmas tree, the boy finds a pile of horse manure. Imagine Dad's surprise when little Jimmy lets out an excited whoop and begins running around the house looking in closets and the backyard. "What are you doing, Jimmy?" Jimmy's reply is in classic sales-speak: "With that much manure, there's got to be a pony in here somewhere!"

Sometimes our sales forecasting looks rosier than it should because we believe there's a pony in there among the manure.

Eeyore Pessimism

We know Eeyore must be popular amongst some salespeople because, despite the indefatigable optimism of many, there is the occasional seller whose forecasts sound as though he is channeling him. A sales Eeyore in a strategy meeting might sound like this:

"Don't have much going on this quarter."

"Smith Companies probably won't close."

"We are very reliant on one guy; I would not be surprised if he got reassigned."

"Abco is probably going to delay until next fiscal year, and I would not be shocked if they went with our competition. Not that it matters."

In our consulting work in the area of forecasting, we've found that it's not just the cock-eyed optimists who screw up their forecasts. Some sellers, when confronted with the optimists' pile of horse manure, would typically shrug and say it's what they expected.

Of course, the doom-and-gloom forecast may be inspired less by a gloomy temperament—or cynicism or even realism—than it is by self-preservation. The sandbagger who downplays his forecast, after all, lowers expectations all around. Instead of seeing gold in "them thar hills," these Eeyores remind everyone how difficult the gold is to extract or how thoroughly mined the hills already are. These gloomy voices would rather keep their forecasts quiet and conservative. No bold promises from them.

Putting our name to a forecast is like making a promise over an outcome we do not directly control. It's uncomfortable. And too many things can turn the "sure thing" into a dead thing.

Very Superstitious

Other salespeople may display a certain reticence about discussing their deals coming to fruition in their forecasts because of deep-seated superstitions.

They're afraid that making an optimistic forecast will jinx the opportunity. So, they are reluctant to say much about it, the way baseball players avoid talking to a pitcher who's throwing a no-hitter.

Of course, when this superstition is examined a bit more closely, we find that it is based on some sound logic. We have worked with many sellers whose greatest worry is that their manager will helicopter into a deal to "move it forward." Late involvement of management may occasionally add to the momentum of an opportunity, but more often, this practice is counterproductive.

Customers do not always respond favorably to the heavy guns being rolled out, likening it to the car dealer who turns you over to the manager for closing the sale. However, there seems to be a strong correlation between a manager's early involvement in—and familiarity with—a customer, and the manager's ability to positively influence the decision.

Sellers who practice "pipeline reticence" are likely worried about the helicopter manager who flies in, raises a lot of dust and noise, and then flies out while the customer runs for cover.

Just as we saw with Susan's and Mike's company, having a clearly defined sales pipeline can quickly improve a company's forecasting accuracy, allow salespeople to be attuned to warning signs of an opportunity stalling or slowing and assist them in responding more appropriately when an opportunity's forward momentum is increased.

Over time, a sales pipeline will help establish reliable metrics that give insights into your business and provide management and stakeholders the accurate forecast they demand.

Clear pipelines make managing complex sales simple enough to make even Eeyore smile.

Chapter 2 Summary

In this chapter, we established the importance of defining the stages of your pipeline process and the required milestones you must meet in order to advance to the next stage. Think about our friend Mike and the first story we told of the opportunity he lost. What did he do wrong during the sales process?

Mike made assumptions during his meeting, which meant he didn't understand where the customer was in their decision-making process. The customer was already at the later stage of the buying process, and Mike's company was brought in simply to justify to higher management why they should opt for using his competitor.

Mike also didn't understand all of the key influencers that were involved in the purchase. He only met with the directors, ignoring or making assumptions that the other people involved in the decision process were less important. Without validating who else was involved and developing a plan to meet with and learn more from other potential influencers, Mike put his opportunity at risk and it cost him.

And finally, he didn't know the decision criteria the company was using to choose whom they wanted to outsource the mailroom to. He didn't know that they were comparing his company to another, and he certainly didn't know why they chose them over him.

Chapter Questions

At the end of each chapter, we provide you with a few questions that might challenge your strategic thinking. The questions below have been developed to help you develop a winning strategy for a current sales opportunity. Read these questions to see if you might be making assumptions or potentially missing some key information.

1. When looking at the strategic milestone in the generic sales process provided in this chapter, which of these milestones do you need to accomplish to better secure a win with your strategically important "must-win" prospect?

2. Think of a current sales opportunity that you are working on. Using the pipeline process we provided in this chapter, are you able to identify where you might place your opportunity in the six stages of the pipeline?

3. When it comes to completing a stage, what can you do to validate that the milestones have been effectively accomplished?

4. Did the description of the snapshot tools reveal any potential gaps in your knowledge about a current or previous account? What could you have done differently?

Selling in today's competitive environment takes a strategic mind, disciplined approach and knowing how to partner with your customer. Ignite Your Sales Strategy focuses salespeople across these domains by challenging their critical thinking and providing easy to use tools to win.

David Brin
Senior Director – Learning Strategy and Operations
GE Healthcare

CHAPTER 3

Understanding Buying Factors

When we were consulting with the company both Mike and Susan work for, our goal was to help the VP of sales achieve the sales goals the board was expecting. The VP of sales shared an assessment his sales enablement team took that identified areas of concern we should address.

The assessment revealed two things to us. First, we found out that his sales team was investing time with potential customers that were not in the market to make a change, therefore wasting time with the wrong prospects.

Second, we found out that the sales team lacked an understanding of customers' key buying factors. They were investing time in selling activities that didn't drive the acceleration of their customers' buying decisions. Both of these challenges were the root cause of why opportunities were stalling in the sales pipeline.

The VP knew the sales reps were working hard but wondered if they were investing time selling smart. After all, just because someone says: "I'm interested in what you have to offer" doesn't mean they're a prospect that you need to be investing time into right now. But how do you know for sure?

As we worked with this tech company, we found out that many of the opportunities the sales team was chasing were getting stalled early in the sales pipeline. They were really struggling with not knowing **why** they were stalling. As we invested time in the field with their sales team and interviewed their sales managers, we found out these were opportunities, in many cases, that should have never been pursued to begin with. The sales team was making too many assumptions around a few key buying factors. So, we sat down with the top ten salespeople in the company to look at their top three opportunities.

As we began digging into the salespeople's top three opportunities, we discovered that they were all in the early to middle stages of their sales pipeline process with opportunities they believed they could close.

We asked them to consider these five factors:

1. The length of the decision-making process.
2. The complexity of the decision-making process.
3. The sense of urgency around making the decision.
4. The consensus among influencers around the decision-making process.
5. Their competitive position.

To help them better understand the value of these five factors, we asked a series of questions that would challenge their assumptions about each opportunity. As we began, we found we were able to expose the reasons why many of these opportunities were stalling in their pipeline process.

To share the results of our assessment with the company, let's visit our friends Mike and Susan and talk about their different experiences. As you read their responses, ask yourself: Are you more like Mike or Susan?

Below are some of the actual responses from our assessment.

Our first question was:

1. What is the length of your customer's decision process for this opportunity? How do you know?

What we found out was that Mike makes a lot of assumptions when approaching a sale. He puts a lot of faith in the Department Head and doesn't validate the information he receives.

When Mike provided us his answer he said, *"They are submitting for budget approval now so we expect to have a decision in the next 3 months."*

After a couple of follow-up questions, such as, *"Did you happen to validate this information with anyone else that is involved in the decision,"* and *"What did the decision process look like last time that made a buying decision like this?"*

Mike responded to both questions quickly, saying that the Head of the Department is someone he can trust and has confidence in the decision timeline.

Susan, on the other hand, did a better job at understanding the length of the decision process. Susan uncovered that past decisions of this magnitude typically go through a buying committee and often require the IT Director to get three bids before submitting them to Procurement. She confirmed this would be the process they would stick with and was told that it would take a minimum of four months before a decision would be made. Having this information allowed Susan to set the proper expectations with both her customer and her sales management team.

In most cases, as well as in this particular scenario, most of the salespeople don't know whether or not their customer's decision-making process is going to be long or short, or what's driving it. They are making assumptions that allow them to believe that all opportunities are good opportunities to invest time into right now. But, simply understanding the length of the customer's decision-making process isn't enough.

So, let's continue with our next questions to Mike and Susan and see the differences between their responses. Our next question was:

2. What's the complexity of their decision process? Is it a highly complex decision-making process your customer needs to make or is this process a real simple decision that only requires a few key influencers?

The interesting fact here was that five of the 10 salespeople we interviewed didn't know the complexity of the decision process. We simply asked if the customer had a standard and consistent process they followed or if they included other factors that could potentially make the decision more complex.

Mike's response to the question was, *"It's likely going to be a fairly simple decision process, they always follow the same protocols for decisions like this."*

Yet, when we encouraged Mike to go back into the account to validate his understanding, he discovered that there was a new Director of Supply Chain and they were going to require the product to be tested onsite for three months before they make any decisions. Mike quickly discovered that his assumptions were incorrect and thus he had to re-adjust his sales forecast.

When we asked Susan the same question, she told us that the decision was going to be made by a committee of 13 different people and it was going to take a few months to get those people together for a meeting. This information allowed Susan to take time to get to know the members of this decision committee and learn more about their business issues and explain how her solution is the best choice for the company.

Too often making assumptions around the complexity of the buying decision prevents salespeople from thinking more strategically. Once the salesperson has an understanding of HOW the decision is going to be made, they can then make better decisions around how they can work to better differentiate their solutions throughout the decision process. The third question we asked was a simple question about assessing the customer's sense of urgency to act. But as we discovered, knowing the level of urgency and what's driving the urgency can be equally important.

3. What is driving the sense of urgency, and is the sense of urgency high or low?

Now, in this case, seven out of 10 salespeople, including both Susan and Mike, knew that there was a HIGH sense of urgency or a moderate sense of urgency to make a change within the company. That wasn't surprising because most salespeople can determine whether or not a customer wants to act now or not. However, when we dug a little further about WHAT was driving the sense of urgency the answers became a little vague.

In Mike's case, he told us the customer's sense of urgency was being driven around the desire to improve departmental efficiencies. When we dug a little further into why improving departmental efficiencies was important *now*, Mike didn't know. If Mike would have known why it was so critical for the department to increase efficiencies he might have been able to better align his capabilities to differentiate his solution from the competition.

Susan shared with us that her client had a high sense of urgency to act now because her client was preparing to launch a new product in a few months and the solution Susan was providing was going to better support those customers. In other words, not having Susan's solution installed could have a negative impact on her client's customer service department. Armed with this information, Susan was able to better align the unique capabilities of her solution to the assets of her client's new product.

The next question we asked was;

4. Is there a consensus around the decision? Is one person able to make the decision or a team of key influencers?

Mike and most of the other salespeople had no idea whether or not there was consensus around the decision. Only one percent of the top 10 salespeople actually knew if there needed to be a consensus around the desire to take action, and that person was Susan.

Mike put all of his eggs in one basket with the Head of the Department. Though he learned the new Director of Supply Chain had some input, he said that the final decision was going to be made by the Department Head.

We asked Mike, "*What has been said or done to make him believe the final decision comes down to the Department Head?*"

He replied, *"the Department Head has always been the key influencer for these solutions."*

That told us that Mike was making an assumption that this decision was simply following the sales decision process of the previous purchase.

When we spoke to Susan about this question, she shared with us that the buying committee of 13 people was simply going with the majority vote. It was going to be a democratic process. This insight helped Susan with her strategy to try and build advocacy amongst as many of the members of the buying committee as possible. And since she knew that it was going to take a couple of months to get everyone together, she had a little time to put her plan into action.

Our final question focused on competitive position:

5. What is your competitive position?

Fortunately, all of the salespeople knew what their competitive position was. Whether or not the client knew them in the past, whether the client was using their solution and whether the client liked their solution or not, all of the salespeople knew at least that. However, like in previous questions, Mike never validated his belief. Mike told us that his prospect has been working with his company for the past seven years, but when we asked if this specific Department Head has worked with his company Mike said no. But he added that his company has always had a great reputation with the CFO.

As you can probably see, this doesn't necessarily validate that Mike's company is in a strong competitive position. Sure, previous success in the account helps, but if the Department Head is unfamiliar with your solutions, there is always some risk, even if he is telling you he likes your products.

Susan, on the other hand, took a more conservative approach when responding to our question. She told us her position is moderate at best. With 13 different influencers, she had some work to do to determine her competitive position. Susan wasn't going to assume that all 13 committee members supported her decision. She wanted to validate and truly understand if each key influencer understood the value of her company and her offering.

As you can see from the responses to these five questions, it's no surprise that the VP of Sales was concerned that his salespeople kept getting stalled. As you read through the questions and reviewed the responses from Mike and Susan, whose response would be more like your own? For most of us, we probably saw a little of Mike and Susan in our responses.

The reality is salespeople are often the eternal optimists and want to find success in any opportunity. But, the reality is that salespeople often fall into the trap of seduction and want to believe the opportunity is real, when in fact if they only spend a little more time validating their understanding they could make a smarter decision regarding the next steps.

Same Old, Same Old? Consistency of the Decision Process

Before we get into each of the five critical buying factors, first we want to show how understanding them can help create a strategy to close the opportunity–and how making assumptions can lead to losing it.

We find that successful salespeople like Susan test their assumptions and understanding around key factors that are going to impact the buying decision. They take nothing for granted. All the old familiar faces may still be in place, but perhaps they have different influences on each decision.

While a formal request for proposal (RFP) process may be the norm for one of your accounts, does that mean there will be one for every opportunity inside that account? Will you be facing the same competitive threat you normally do, or will a new competitive threat emerge? What does the competition bring to the table this time?

If you approach a new opportunity with old eyes you run the risk of making too many assumptions, missing key information and not putting yourself in the best position to win.

Let's use one of Susan's experiences here to give you an example.

Susan was working hard to close an opportunity with a national hospital chain to get them to purchase equipment, software and the professional services her tech company offered. Her competitor, however, was king in this specific product category throughout most of the hospitals across the region.

Both Susan and her competitor understood that the customer was interested in improving the equipment and enhancing the software in all of their operating rooms. The sense of urgency in this sale was high, and the length of the decision process seemed low. This hospital was going to make a decision fairly quickly.

Both Susan and her competitor developed a compelling argument about why they each deserved to be the solution provider for the hospital.

But the competitor's salesperson assumed the new decision process would be consistent with the way decisions had always been made before. In the past, the Chief Nursing Officer would pilot the solution in several hospitals across the region and see what kind of returns they would get from the ORs.

In this case, the Chief Nursing Officer was familiar with both companies' solutions and the marketing strategy from both companies. So they did a phone survey of a selected group of hospitals in the region and made the decision based on the feedback from the selected OR Directors. Because the process had changed, it introduced new influencers into the buying process.

Fortunately, Susan had found out about this approach ahead of time, so she was able to contact several of the hospitals prior to the Chief Nursing Officer conducting their own survey. Conducting her own research allowed Susan to build a consensus among the OR Directors (influencers), and she developed a smarter strategy to help local OR Directors see the value in her product.

At the end of the day, she won the hospital's business because she didn't assume the decision process was going to be the same as before and, she considered each buying factor before forming her strategy.

The average-performing salespeople would make the assumption that all the buying factors that were in place during a previous sale will also be in place during the current sale. With this assumption, our average performer, Mike, would not even be bothered to validate the complexity of the sale, develop a plan to manage the influencers, or simply ask the Chief Nursing Officer what the decision process will look like. Mike would simply assume that the hospital system would follow similar buying protocols they've used in the past.

It's no wonder that the VP of Sales for this company was finding opportunities stalling in the sales pipeline!

The Five Key Factors

Let's continue by diving deeper into the **five critical factors underlying all customer's buying processes**. The first component of thinking and acting strategically is understanding these five factors and how to influence them in your favor.

All of these factors are interrelated and reveal a complete picture of what strategic actions need to be taken to get the customer to make the buying decision in your favor. While we'll consider them individually in order to fully explain them, none of them should be considered in isolation. While there is some utility in categorizing them, looking at them in isolation would be like looking at the world through a straw. And although we present them in sequence, it would be false to say they must be addressed in the same sequence.

We see top-performers consider each set of factors independently but with a careful eye as to how they interact with each other. For example, an opportunity with a short decision process, high sense of urgency and multiple decision-makers might unfold quite a bit differently than one with a long cycle, low sense of urgency and fewer decision-makers.

Are We Done Yet? The Length of the Decision Process

The first factor contributing to a successful strategy has to do with knowing how long it's going to take for the customer to decide whether or not to buy your solution.

Just as a marathon consumes the runner's energy over a long period, so too does a lengthy decision cycle consume your resources. You'll need to pace yourself in order to have enough energy for the end of the race.

A lengthy cycle requires equal parts patience and persistence. You'll need to stay connected to your advocates, keep your fingers on the customer's pulse and watch for signs of change. The savvy salesperson also needs to keep their resources at the ready, held in reserve for the final kick at the finish.

On the other hand, a shorter cycle is more like a sprint. It's all muscle and adrenaline, with lots of energy consumed in a rapid burst. Finishing a sprint demands that you align resources as quickly as possible and know just when and how to use them. The average performer will haphazardly throw resources, such as research, client references and senior sales executives into the sales process in a desperate attempt to win the sale.

For example, Susan, our top performer, was working with a grocery store chain to replace all of their outdated inventory systems with her company's technology. The chain was consistently losing money due to the mistakes their old system made and it was no longer advantageous to try and patch the existing software. The system had to be replaced.

Susan spoke with several managers at the stores and found out that even though they were losing money with the older system, they were still dragging their feet to find a replacement because they knew they would have to train all their employees on the new technology. It was going to be a huge burden.

Susan started developing a strategy around emphasizing the ease of use of her solution, taking her time to develop it because she thought that the sense of urgency for the buying process was low.

While she was researching the store manager's specific pain points, she learned that there had been a change in plan. The CFO of the grocery chain set a hard deadline on approving the budget for the upgrade by the end of the fiscal year, only five weeks away, and needed the managers to decide on a solution sooner rather than later.

Now that she knew the length of the decision process was much shorter, she quickly adapted her strategy. Susan acted fast in positioning her resources and strengthening her competitive position. She was able to meet the CFO's deadline more effectively than her competition, ultimately winning the sale.

How Hard Could It Be? Validating the Complexity of the Decision Process

Top performers work very hard to understand the complexity of the customer's buying process in order to develop a strategy that positions their solution best.

They answer questions like: What is the process my customer uses to make their purchasing decisions? Does it involve a formal proposal? A decision committee? A single decision-maker? Budget approval from a board of directors? Is it different from similar buying decisions they've made in the past? If so, how?

They do this because top performers know that the **complexity of the customer's decision process will affect your sales strategy.**

With a complex decision process, you'll want to make sure you're on top of following the customer protocols, like submitting the correct paperwork on time, and engaging the right people at the right time, all to ensure there isn't a negative impact on your sale.

If your typical sale has more than one influencer, it boosts the level of complexity because you have to build a consensus with more people and establish your competitive position with them.

Our friend Susan's experiences relate to this. She was working with a large distribution center that was redesigning their computer stations and needed new technology in 17 different locations of the warehouse.

As she worked through her opportunity strategy, her manager pointed out that she was overlooking three critical influencers. Apparently, two people Susan hadn't even considered were members of a special committee charged with improving operational efficiencies within the distribution center.

This special committee was formed by the corporate headquarters and included a few department heads. Because Susan didn't typically engage that level until later in her sales process, she hadn't considered their role in the decision process to be so important early on. This obviously made the customer's decision process a bit more complex.

Susan was able to use this recommendation from her manager to change her strategy. Susan developed a plan to understand the key drivers of the department heads and what steps they had taken up to this point to improve their business metrics. She learned that she could improve efficiencies at the loading dock that would have a great impact further up the supply chain.

Because she took her manager's advice, she was able to demonstrate the value at a higher level than her competition and thus she was selected as the solution partner of choice.

However, simply understanding the complexity of the buying process and developing a smart strategy to align your solutions is not enough. Top performers realize that they must connect how each influencer in the decision defines the problem and thus how your solution can help. When a customer's decision process includes multiple decision-makers, this requires people to slow down and think before they simply start to take action.

Where's the Fire? Finding or Creating a Sense of Urgency

The next critical factor underlying the customer's buying process is their sense of urgency. Like we mentioned before, most salespeople understand whether or not a customer wants to act now or not. But sometimes the customer's sense of urgency is either unclear or unknown.

As one of our clients once told us, "Sometimes we're lucky and the sense of urgency driving the decision is internal, and all you have to do is hang on and work to influence the decision in your favor." Just like a roller coaster. For other opportunities, we have to create a sense of urgency. "If there's no burning platform, we have to light one on fire."

One of the experiences Mike shared with us demonstrates the importance of understanding your potential customer's sense of urgency.

Mike was working with a regional retail chain to replace over 300 of their inventory management systems with his company's new system and processes. Mike was fortunate to get his solution approved for trial and the trial process was a success, so naturally, he thought he had the sale in the bag.

However, as the weeks went by he struggled to get access to his contacts at the retailer headquarters. After three weeks passed, Mike finally managed to speak with his contact. He learned that the plan to replace the inventory management systems was now on hold.

Mike was confused. How could the committee put the project on hold after putting forth all the effort to evaluate a new solution? Mike soon learned that the company had just hired a new CFO, someone who had a reputation for scrutinizing every spending decision.

So, what can he do now? Wait until they feel ready to re-engage? Mike knew that the retail store managers preferred his solution over the competition. However, if Mike was a highly motivated top performer and driver, he would have known he had to find a way to create a sense of urgency to get the company to take action now.

A top performer would find or create a sense of urgency to get the deal back on track. They would schedule a meeting with the new CFO, using their advocate inside the company to arrange an introduction. They would listen to the CFO's plans and objectives related to profitability. Then, they would demonstrate how their company's track record aligned with the CFO's objectives, specifically demonstrating the link between their solution's key strengths and those key metrics that were important to the CFO.

Mike assumed that just because he knew the retail store managers preferred his solution over his competitor's, it would only be a matter of time before he closed the deal. This mindset eventually led to Mike losing the opportunity because his competitor found a way to light a fire and create a sense of urgency to get the retail chain to go with their system instead.

An average performer, like Mike, makes the assumption that because a customer has high urgency to fix a problem then the decision will be made quickly and in the simplest way. But, what average performers fail to take into account is that the client may be moving towards the decision as quickly as they can given any restrictions the company may have in place.

He would also assume that because one person in the organization expressed a high sense of urgency, then that feeling is mutual for everyone else in the organization, when really that may not be the case.

So, in this scenario, Mike could have worked to gain a sense of the customer's urgency and continued to keep the retail chain in his favor with that information.

Of course, even with a high sense of urgency, salespeople still have to work to drive the client to make the change, and also consider any and all restrictions the customer may have to work with when deciding on their purchase.

There are some sales opportunities that remind us of roller coasters. As one of our clients told us, "Sometimes we're lucky and the sense of urgency driving the decision is internal, and all you have to do is hang on and work to influence the decision in your favor." Just like a roller coaster.

For other opportunities, we have to create a sense of urgency. As one executive told us, "If there's no burning platform, we have to light one on fire."

Some questions that will help you determine your customer's sense of urgency include:

- What's driving your customer's decision to act?
- Is there a driving force in the market forcing them to act now?
- Does each influencer have the same sense of urgency?

It would be great if your opportunity was the only one on the customer's radar. Unfortunately, that's only true in our sales fantasies. Many other projects are competing for the attention, to say nothing of the time and money, of our customers.

Moreover, we are not the only ones buzzing in our customers' ears. Sometimes, these decisions represent a zero-sum game; when one wins approval, other solutions or other projects altogether are immediately put on the back burner. Part of our challenge is keeping the customer's focus on us and convincing them that our product is important to their overall success.

All For One – Solution: Building Consensus Among Influencers

Identifying all the potential influencers, both those for us and those against us, is a big step in understanding the customers' buying factors. Questions like: What are their roles in the decision process, how much influence do they actually have, and which of those influencers support our solutions and which ones don't, all help to organize your strategy in building a consensus among them.

We spend a substantial amount of time discussing these questions in the next chapter. For now, when you are assessing the factors underlying a buying decision, it's just about headcount: Who are the influencers and what role do they play?

While being able to identify the key influencers involved in a buying decision is critical, merely knowing "who's who in the zoo" isn't enough. The critical best practice, of course, is actually **building a consensus of opinion around the decision.** Building consensus requires being able to answer two key questions.

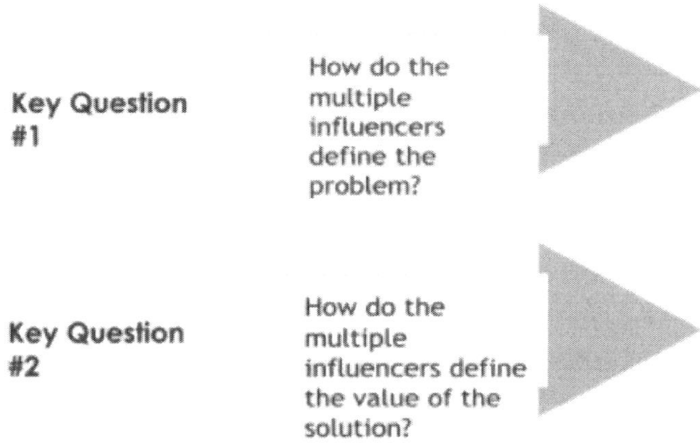

First, you must have clarity regarding how the multiple buyers define the problem. Second, you need clarity about how the multiple buyers define value in the solution.

In Susan's case, if the buyers didn't agree about which new technology they should replace first, the decision could have been delayed or the plan could have been totally scrapped. Fortunately for Susan, she was able to give the key influencers a common understanding of the problem and the desire to fix it.

The Usual Suspects? Know the Competition and Their Strengths

The last critical factor you have to consider is **determining your competitive position**. Knowing who you're up against in the customer's eyes is key to a successful sale.

We have all been victims of a "trick play"–we lose a deal because someone behind the scenes preferred our competition. When this happens we may make excuses for ourselves or cry foul. But the truth of the matter is that we just did not notice them or under-estimated the position of the competitor in the eyes of the key influencer(s). They were right there, standing on the sidelines.

We learned this the hard way during one of our own sales. We had an opportunity to provide a sales strategy solution to a global cloud technology company. The solution would have been about a half a million-dollar opportunity, a large sale for our company. Unfortunately, we lost to a good competitor.

Doing a postmortem on this lost opportunity was painful, but eye-opening for us. We broke down every element of our strategy, discovering the reason we lost was simply because we'd underestimated our competitive position.

We poorly assumed that our unique capabilities to provide a simulation-based approach, our global experience to deliver training in multiple languages and our proven large-scale implementation methods were enough to win against this "less experienced" and "less qualified" competitor. We also assumed that the previous relationship our competitor had with one of the major key influencers wasn't enough to sway the decision in their favor.

We were wrong on all accounts. Our competitive position wasn't as strong as we had assumed. During our postmortem, we realized that since our competitive position was weak we could have tried to leverage our relationship with the VP of Sales. We'd met with him in the past and we knew he believed our solution was a great fit for his sales team. Instead, we put our faith in a few people in the Sales Enablement Department and assumed our competitive position was enough. Overall, it was a very poor decision.

We all can fall into the trap of complacency, believing our competitive position is stronger than it actually is. Sometimes falling into the trap of assuming that all of the key influencers in the decision understand our unique value and why it's a better decision to do business with us over the competition. Slowing down and examining your strategy several times is always a good idea.

Let's look at another sales opportunity our friend Susan had success with while we were working with her. Susan had a strong customer relationship that she'd been developing for over five years. The customer was worth about $4 million annually to Susan's company, which was about 30 percent of Susan's annual quota.

Susan's customer wanted to centralize much of the inventory into one single distribution center and provide just in time inventory services to their customer, but they were struggling to get regional offices to comply.

The regional offices preferred to keep inventory local for a diverse range of reasons. They were extremely loyal to their local customers, with many of them having community and personal ties. It didn't take a detective to realize that buying from these regional offices would be very tough indeed. Moreover, Susan's customer was reluctant to stiff-arm the regional offices to get on board with the plan. A winning strategy would have to provide a win-win approach.

Instead of positioning herself as their competition, Susan worked to be an ally with the regional offices. She could offer regional offices the best of both worlds, which meant that they could maintain inventory for those commonly used disposable items, but the main distribution center would maintain inventory for everything else and Susan's company would provide the solution for all locations.

This "alliance" approach allowed regional offices to maintain control of the disposable inventory and feel as if they could still provide the local service and support their customer's expectations, while at the same time satisfying the corporate interest to manage more of the total inventory to save on inventory cost and overall spend. Susan's success was the result of identifying who her competition was and then formulating a strategy based on their strengths and weaknesses.

Then What? The Situational Snapshot®

Now that you have a better understanding of customer buying factors, it's time to input what you know into the Situational Snapshot®.

The Situational Snapshot® is a tool to help you better understand the key buying factors impacting the opportunity. It's a picture of your strategic position for a given sales opportunity at a given point in time.

It will help you assess your strategic position, prioritize your actions by determining the strength or weakness of each buying factor, recognize the relationship between the buying factors and analyze how shifts in any factor impact the whole snapshot.

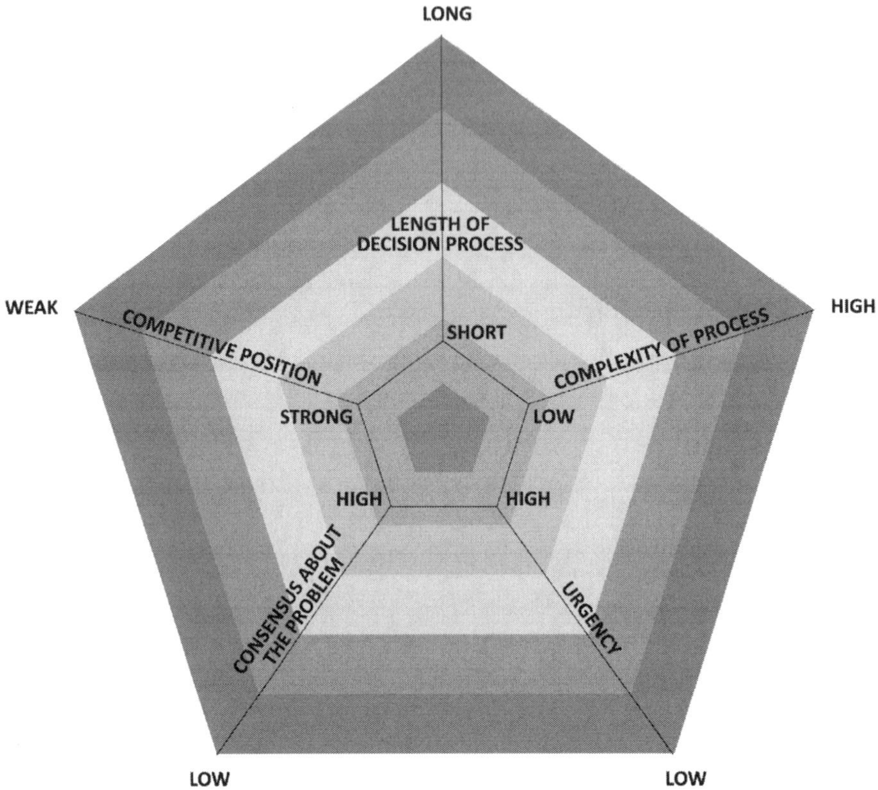

The green area represents your most favorable position on the snapshot, while the red area represents your least favorable position for each buying factor.

Each of the buying factors rests on an axis that ranges from low to high, short to long and weak to strong. You'll plot your position on each axis to create a picture of your strategic position. Once you have your strategic position, you can create a strategy that addresses each aspect of the customers buying factors.

Now, the Situational Snapshot® is not written in stone, so keep in mind that as a single factor changes, the others might shift as well. If you find out an opportunity has more competitors than you thought or there are more influencers involved in the decision process, the length of the decision process is also likely to change.

You'll have to come back to and re-evaluate and update your positions as your sale evolves. Keeping it up to date will assist in managing the sale effectively.

Chapter 3 Summary

In this chapter, we introduced a tool called the Situational Snapshot® which helps visualize how an opportunity stands against five critical buying factors. Understanding these buying factors and determining how to influence them in your favor is the key to thinking and acting strategically as you navigate your sales opportunities. Think about what your customer might want, why they want it, when they want it and what motivates them to get it.

The five key components are:

- Knowing the length of the customer decision process.
- Determining the level of complexity in the decision process and what's driving it.
- Finding, or creating, a sense of urgency within the customer.
- Identifying if there's a consensus between the key influencer(s) around the buying decision.
- Knowing your competitive position based upon who your competition is.

Let's circle back to our friend Mike. Mike didn't have an understanding of some of his customer's key buying factors. He assumed that if something was true in the past it will still be true in the future. So, simply because Mike was in a strong competitive position and had built up a lot of rapport with influencers during a previous opportunity—he believed that his position and those relationships still stood.

But as we now know, this is not always the case. Mike's position changed and the people who were influential previously weren't influential anymore. Not confirming this information beforehand is part of why Mike didn't close the opportunity.

Mike could have a champion or friend within the organization to tell him if his competitive position was strong or not. But Mike, without verifying this information, assumed that everyone in the company felt the same way about his solution. By underestimating the importance of each buying factor, his competitor was able to come along and win the sale, leaving Mike confused about how he let the opportunity slip from his fingers.

Notice how if even one of the five factors changes, it influences the other factors as well. When Susan was selling her technology solution to the regional hospital system and found out about the special committee, it not only made the complexity of the sale go up, it also lengthened the decision process.

Chapter Questions

These questions are designed to engage you in understanding your customer's buying factors and help you develop a complete and accurate Situational Snapshot®. Like in the previous chapter, think of a current sales opportunity you are working on, and ask yourself these questions;

1. What has been said that makes you believe the customer's decision process is either long or short?
2. Does there need to be consensus around this decision, or are differing opinions around making a change OK? If you need consensus to make a change, what is your first step in making this happen?
3. What have you done to validate the sense of urgency around making a change in their current systems? If the urgency is LOW to MODERATE, what can you do to increase the sense of urgency, and who can help you? If the buying decision is highly complex, what three actions do you need to take to ensure your solution is best aligned to how this customer is going to make a decision?
4. What are two things you can do to strengthen your competitive position for this opportunity?
5. When considering the five buying factors in the Situational Snapshot®, what assumptions might you be making, and how can you validate your understanding?

Salespeople spend too much time in their comfort zone, focusing on those individuals that like them, hoping they can carry their solution across the finish line. Ignite Your Sales Strategy provides an easy-to-use set of tools to help salespeople proactively identify key influencers and develop proactive strategies to leverage advocates and neutralize adversaries. When salespeople stop assuming who the key influencers are and what's driving their desire to change or not change, the net result can be more sales and successful implementations.

Heather Fraser
Executive Director
Global Investment Banking Company

CHAPTER 4

Managing Key Influencers

When discussing key influencers, we are not talking about the opposition or our enemies. We are speaking of our **customers**. We want to win their favor, not defeat them.

In this chapter, we will be talking about managing the key influencers in your targeted accounts. A successful salesperson will invest time to understand the business challenges and metrics their customers are being held accountable for. We want to know their ups and downs, their ins and outs. We want to know who they are, what they want and why they want it.

Knowing the key influencers in your accounts is important, but knowing how to leverage or manage those key influencers to support a buying decision in your favor is crucial for success. This chapter, while not providing a magic bullet to make handling the key influencers easy (or always successful), will nevertheless give you a useful tool and proven best practices to make it manageable.

Lots of Cooks in the Kitchen!

Complex sales are complex. Avoid the temptation to dismiss this point simply because it states the obvious. The complexity we speak of here relates to the number of people inside an organization who have the ability to influence major purchasing decisions.

Our research indicates that companies have become more careful and calculated when it comes to making major purchasing decisions. Companies are more diligent about assessing the economic impact of the purchase, more regimented in their evaluation of competing alternatives, and lastly, are engaging more people in the decision-making process through the use of decision or value analysis committees. It is far rarer these days to see a complex sales situation where only one or two people are involved in making the final decision.

Therefore, it is critical for salespeople to have a complete grasp of the key influencer situation for each sales opportunity they are pursuing and to develop effective strategies to effectively manage those key influencers.

Let's visit our friend Mike again. One of Mike's biggest customers was a large manufacturing and distribution operation. Mike had managed the relationship for five years and had developed good relationships with some of the more vocal users in the account. When the company announced it was making an investment in a new inventory management system, Mike thought the deal was his. After all, Mike already had some proven technology embedded inside the company and his inventory management solution was preferred by those same key users Mike liked so much.

Three months later, to Mike's surprise, he lost the deal.

In hindsight, Mike realized that he had made two key mistakes. First, he vastly overestimated the level of advocacy his "friends" in the account held toward him and his solutions. Sure, they liked him and they liked his products, but they were not "disciples" of his solutions who would reliably go out and spread the word to others. In fact, when asked, those individuals provided mixed reviews of Mike's solutions — highlighting both the things they liked (ease of use and reliability) and the things they didn't like (expansion options and price).

The second mistake Mike made was to put too much energy into his relationships with a few key users. The people Mike had developed a good relationship with had always, in the past, exerted a great deal of influence over the decision-making process. Mike assumed those individuals would exert the same amount of influence this go around. Mike really thought he knew everyone he needed to know inside the account, but he later learned that his competitor was actually engaging people in different departments and speaking about the value of their solution in a different way.

The tough part for Mike is that his situation was avoidable. All he had to do was stop assuming and instead ask some simple questions, such as: "Other than yourself, who else is involved in the decision this time? Who has the most influence in *this* specific purchasing decision?"

In sales, if you don't know who your competition is speaking to, you are likely putting this opportunity at risk of failing. Mike's strategy was to continue to work with his champion to advance his sales efforts. He hoped his advocate would promote his solution to the other key influencers in the organization.

Mike also acknowledged the need to proactively address his "enemy"— those adversaries that seem to prefer the competitors' solution over his own — and he had a couple of ideas as to how. One approach was to use his advocates to directly confront the adversaries, to use his friend to build credibility for his company and solutions. A second, albeit far less serious option, was a dark alley confrontation with Mike to remove his adversaries from the picture, though all kidding aside, when he thought it through, neither plan filled him with confidence. In reality, it showed that he really lacked a plan. But why?

Mike, like many other sellers, liked to rely on people he was comfortable with. He preferred to focus his efforts on "friends" rather than "enemies." If his friends were more influential than his enemies, he tended to win. If not, he tended to lose. Given that he typically had more friends than enemies, he usually won more than he lost. The downside, of course, was that he might lose opportunities he could easily win.

Another reason Mike's plan was lacking has to do with human nature. Most people tend to avoid confrontations. Mike was no different. Calling directly on his adversaries was almost unthinkable for Mike. Why would he? It might result in a disagreement, which would certainly be counterproductive. Better to let his friend do his fighting for him in this case. Most salespeople prefer to let their advocates carry their banner for them, having no real strategy for counteracting or neutralizing apparent enemies such as Mike's.

Selling only inside our "comfort zones" has other downsides, the most prominent being how our perspective on the situation tends to be skewed. We only hear one side of the story, and it may be woefully inadequate. Another downside is that our advocates may be less influential than we realize. It's not that they can't help us at all, but maybe they can't help us enough. We ought not to put all of our eggs into one basket as Mike attempted.

Now let's talk about Susan, who was involved in a similar situation with one of her accounts. When Susan first learned about the opportunity (this time for an order management software solution), she started engaging with those individuals with whom she had good relationships due to the work she'd been doing inside the account.

However, Susan engaged with these individuals differently. Instead of trying to "sell" her solution to these individuals, she first started to use them to help her gain a complete understanding of the other key influencers who would be involved in this specific decision-making process. Susan began to ask questions about who was really involved in the decision-making process and what role they played in the process.

Through her questions, Susan learned that some of the same people from the last decision were indeed involved again. In addition, Susan discovered there were a few new people engaged in the process this time around. Some of the people she'd worked with in the last purchasing decision had become more influential and some had become less influential.

Because she's a top performer, Susan did not assume. She asked questions.

After gaining the information she needed to build an accurate Influencer Snapshot® Susan actually took the completed Snapshot® tool to her strongest advocate and said, "I have a diagram here showing who I believe has high/low influence for this particular decision, and how those individuals feel about my solution. What do you think? Is my assessment accurate?" Susan simply painted the picture and the customer made the necessary corrections and adjustments. The customer said, "No, this person doesn't have as much influence as you think, *this* person has a higher level of influence." In this case, Susan completed a critical milestone by getting a complete and accurate Influencer Snapshot® created for the opportunity. With a complete and accurate picture, Susan was able to develop a proactive strategy to leverage her advocates to help neutralize her adversaries.

In the end, in a competitive bid situation, Susan won the opportunity because she hit the pause button so she could think more strategically, validated her understanding of the key influencers and asked her advocates for help on how to neutralize any adversaries.

It's important to recognize that over time, influencers can change, and they can change in importance. What becomes critical is staying on top of the new influencers; not just by name and title but by the *level of influence over the decisions being made too.*

Back to the Drawing Board

Bob Ross is a famous painter, art instructor and television host. People of a certain age, including us, remember him for the television show The Joy of Painting, which ran for 12 years on PBS. Ross joyfully painted scenic landscapes, usually filled with "happy little trees."

Apart from his own personal charm, what made the show interesting was the way he created the painting. Beginning with the background, he added layer upon layer, moving toward the foreground. Just when you thought he was done, he added another layer, which made the painting richer and more detailed.

Building a sales strategy is much like Bob Ross and his paintings. The "picture" you will create is a graphical and narrative depiction of how your customer is going to make their decision. Having it on hand will allow you to determine an appropriate strategy for moving forward.

Beginning with the background, you add layer upon layer until you have a clear and detailed picture. Key influencers are part of that background. Who should be included? Obviously, not every person is an influencer, because not everyone inside your customer's organization is involved in every decision. Each situation is different, so each picture will be different. Those who need to be included in your picture are those who are involved in and have influence over a decision. This could be anyone, frankly, and depends upon many factors that change from sale to sale.

It's been our experience that not all key influencers will be recognizable as such, nor will you necessarily know them by name or title. Top performers, like our friend Susan, tend to ask the question, "Who will be involved in the decision?" early in the sales process. By casting a wide net at the beginning of the sales process, top performers can avoid being blindsided by the influence of an unknown individual.

Painting Your Masterpiece

The Influencer Snapshot® is a simple, easy-to-use strategy development tool designed to give you a visual image of the key influencers for a given sales opportunity. There are three steps to building a complete and accurate Influencer Snapshot®.

Step #1 – Who Is Involved?

First, identify all individuals who may potentially play a role. Consider not only those you know by name but also functional areas. For example, if you do not personally know anyone in procurement but are certain someone will be involved, list "procurement."

Along with the customer's internal team, consider whether external resources might be involved, such as consultants or partners. Try not to eliminate any key influencer that might have input in the decision.

Step #2 – How Do They Feel About You?

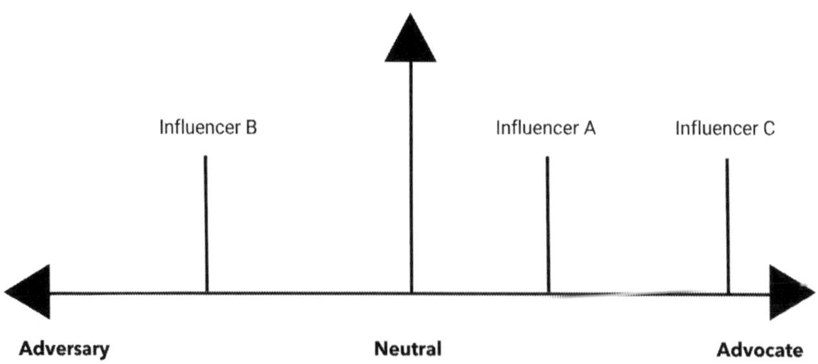

The second step is to consider how each of these influencers feels about you and your solution, especially when compared to our competition. What is their temperature? Are they for us? Against us? Somewhere in between? Each influencer can be assessed on the Advocacy scale, which measures from an Extreme Advocate on one end of the scale to an Extreme Adversary on the other.

To help accurately place influencers on this Advocacy scale, it helps to understand the behaviors exhibited by someone who would be considered at one extreme or the other. Extreme Advocates are our best friends inside the account. These individuals can do a lot to help us inside an account, including the following:

- Fight for our solutions
- Speak positively to others inside the account
- Provide insights (about influencers, competitors, etc.) to help us develop a better strategy
- Help us navigate their company's purchasing process
- Assess our strategy and help us prevent mistakes

Salespeople frequently overestimate someone's advocacy for their solution. Don't make the assumption that just because someone uses your product or solution, they are an advocate. They may just be someone who likes your product, but they are not willing to go speak to others on your behalf. Ask yourself: How much of a preference does this person have for us over our competitors? Are they a raving fan (tough to find, by the way, and not always a good thing)? What actions could I ask this person to take that could help me win the opportunity?

Extreme Adversaries, on the other hand, are standing in our way. These individuals are taking actions to keep us from succeeding, such as:

- Actively campaigning against us or our solutions
- Introducing new layers of complexity that highlight our weaknesses
- Highlighting our competitive weaknesses (true or not) to other key influencers
- Creating doubt about our ability to deliver

Just because someone is behaving like an Extreme Adversary, doesn't necessarily mean they are in the opposite corner with your competition. In fact, they may be trying to shut the fight down altogether. When you've identified an Extreme

Adversary, it is important to take the steps necessary to determine why they seem to want to see us lose. Are they a raving fan of the competition? Do they have a project or budget that would be hindered by our progress?

Most people you encounter as an influencer in a sales opportunity don't act as if they are on the extreme ends of the Advocacy scale. This is particularly true when individuals have formed an official decision committee. Generally speaking, people on committees want to appear to others on the committee as objective and open-minded about the decision, even if they secretly harbor preference. It is easy to mistake these individuals as advocates just because they are pleasant to you. Keep in mind, they might be pleasant to everyone! In order to accurately assess a person's level of advocacy, you have to test them and test their loyalty and preferences. You have to ask questions and explore their experiences. And, more importantly, you have to validate their behaviors with others who are your extreme advocates. You have to know what is going on behind the scenes, and your Extreme Advocate is your best resource.

Step #3 – Are They Influential?

The third step involved in building an accurate Influencer Snapshot® is to assess each individual's influence over the decision. A person's level of influence in a specific decision-making process is a factor of a person's ability (position, credibility, respect by others, engagements in past decisions, etc.) to influence and impact a person's willingness (motivation, engagement, passion, etc.) to influence. Salespeople often make the mistake of only assessing a person's level of influence based on ability, and while ability is a key factor, it isn't the only element that needs to be considered.

A final thing to consider regarding influence is that you have to assess each person's influence relative to the others who are involved in the process. If you have five influencers involved in the decision-making process, you have to assess them against one another to essentially stack rank them from 1 to 5. Although lots of people like to argue this fact, no two people can exert the same amount of influence in a decision-making process. Even though the difference between two peoples' levels of influence may be minuscule, there is still a difference. To unearth the difference between two peoples' levels of influence, you need to ask comparison questions, such as:

- "I know both people have a lot of say in this. If only one could get their way, who would it be?"

- "Does Person A or Person B appear to be more vocal in their opinions?"
- "I know Tom and Mary are both VPs, but whose opinion does the AVP respect more?"

We can use a similar scale to map a key player's influence in a specific decision-making process, from High Influence to Low Influence:

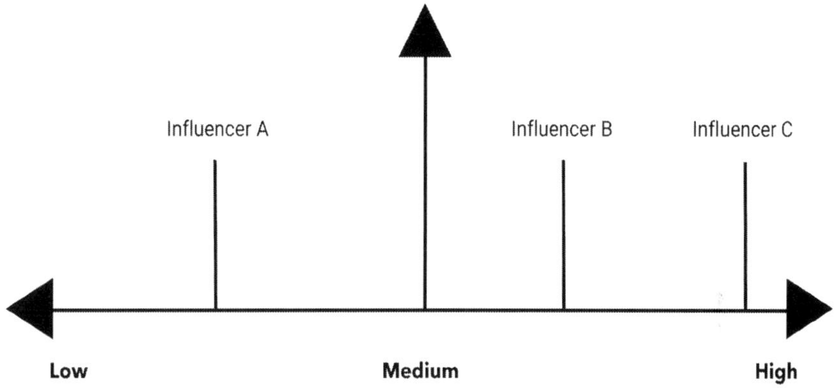

Remember, the measure of someone's influence is specific to the opportunity at hand. A person's influence may wax or wane, depending on many factors, including but not limited to his title and function. Someone who has a position of authority, such as CFO, may or may not opt to exert that influence over the decision. It is important to avoid assuming that anyone with a position of power will also carry a high level of influence. Remember: Influence is based on a person's **ability** and **willingness** to influence others.

A final point to remember is that a person's level of influence in a specific decision is relative to others engaged in the process. As we stated earlier, no two people will have the same level of influence; one person or the other will always be slightly higher or slightly lower. There are never two "head chefs," never two "head coaches."

Sure, there may be two assistant head coaches or two Area Vice Presidents. But when you start assessing the level of influence, you have to factor in a number of things to help you come up with your final assessment that ultimately becomes the stack ranked order the key influencers have over the decision-making process.

Picking Up Your Brush: The Influencer Snapshot®

Now that you know the three steps required to build an accurate Influencer Snapshot®, it's time to put your Influencer Snapshot® together.

The Influencer Snapshot's® two-by-two matrix helps salespeople **better leverage the key influencers involved in the buying decision.** The vertical axis maps the level of influence each influencer has on the buying decision, while the horizontal axis represents where you stand with your influencers. Combine these two simple scales, as shown in the figure on the following page.

When you complete the Influencer Snapshot® you will find a "picture" that is unique to the situation in which you are working.

Creating your sketch of the key influencers seems simple, doesn't it? Yet appearances can be deceiving. Like Bob Ross and his famous paintings, just when you think it's done, it's not. Populating the Influencer Snapshot® tool is a simple task. But that doesn't mean it's easy.

In a perfect situation, you have the knowledge and insights to complete the Influencer Snapshot® accurately. However, in many situations, particularly early in the sales process, completing the tool involves some guesswork about where folks lie along the spectrums. Beware of making too many assumptions about where people fall on the Influencer Snapshot® because your assumptions may very well turn out to be wrong. To get it right, you will need to continually validate your thinking with those closest to the decision.

Knowing how things stand with key influencers is always advantageous, if not always comforting. But even if this mapping process reveals how poor your situation is, it at least allows you to understand where you are.

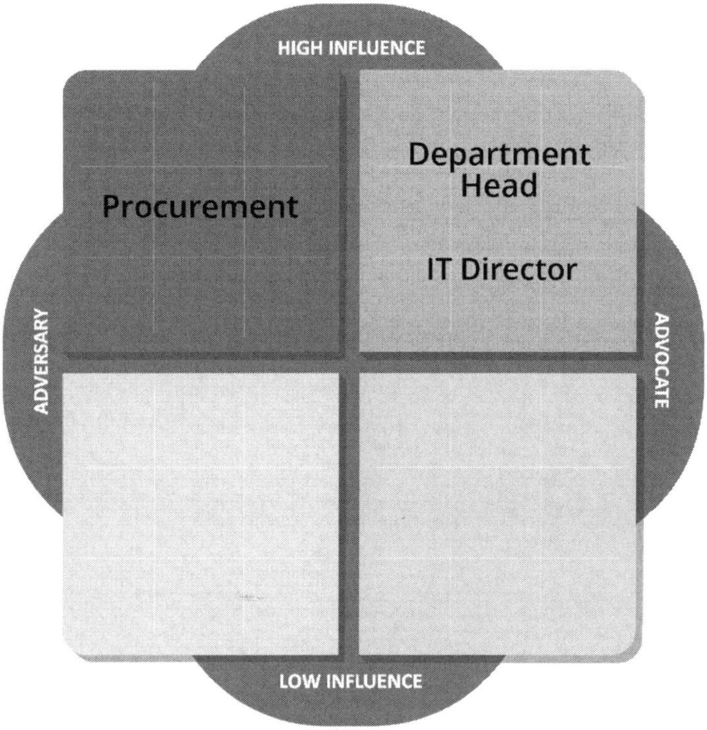

The image above represents Mike's original Influencer Snapshot®.

We put this concept to work with our friend Mike. In order to get a more complete picture of the decision-makers and influencers, we asked Mike to complete an Influencer Snapshot® for one of his prospective accounts. We even included Mike's advocate in the discussion, mostly because we believed Mike lacked a real understanding of who might actually influence the decision.

The Influencer Snapshot® looked a lot different after the discussion. In the original version Mike completed, there were only three people listed. After the conversation with the customer, there were six people included. If Mike had only worked off of his own assumptions, he would have completely ignored half of the total number of influencers inside the account. The dialogue with his key advocate helped Mike have a more complete understanding of who was involved in the decision process and how they felt about Mike's solution.

Unfortunately, the complete (and accurate) Influencer Snapshot® showed he was in a poor position inside the account. There were too many highly influential people who weren't advocates of Mike's solution. Although his picture looked grim, at least Mike had gained a better understanding of where he stood. With that understanding, Mike could now develop a strategy that might actually work.

You've Drawn the Picture. Now What?

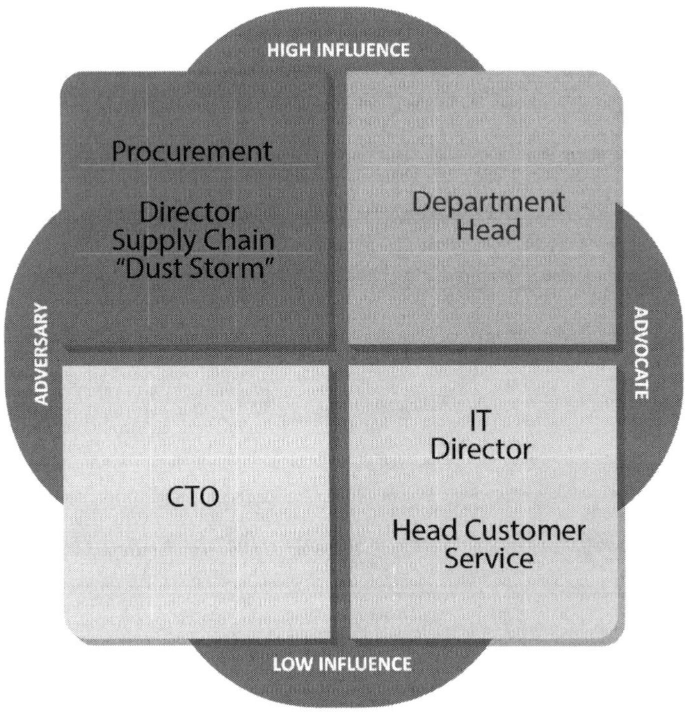

The image above represents Mike's Influencer Snapshot® after his coaching session.

Research on sales planning is pretty clear: There is not a significant amount of difference between average and successful performers when it comes to the time spent developing a strategy. Average performers and top performers tend to spend about the same amount of time on it. What is different is how they spend their time. Average performers, like Mike, tend to emphasize gathering information, while top performers, like Susan, tend to emphasize what to do with it. Put another way, average performers spend the majority of their time figuring out what they want, while top performers spend the majority of their time figuring out how they are going to get what they want. In the simplest of terms, you might say this is the difference between preparation and planning.

Putting the Influencer Snapshot® together is preparation. Putting together effective movement strategies to change the Influencer Snapshot® is planning. What does successful planning look like? Let's first define what we're calling a "Movement Strategy." A movement strategy is a proactive executable plan that improves your picture or situation in the opportunity. It could be as easy as taking a moderate advocate and turning them into a stronger supporter of your solution. Let's consider a few other potential Movement Strategies for the Influencer Snapshot®.

Strengthening Your Position

Certainly, the greatest objective when looking at your Influencer Snapshot® is to determine ways to tip the scale in your favor. To most people, that means figuring out how to turn everyone into an advocate. On the Influencer Snapshot®, that would mean pushing people as far to the right on the Advocacy scale as you can. Unfortunately, while turning everyone into a strong Advocate is a noble quest, it is probably an unrealistic objective. Let's face it; some people are adversaries - for whatever reason. It could be that they had a bad past experience with your product. It could be they just don't like you or your company. Or, it could be that they are adversarial to everyone. Therefore, you are going to need a few alternative movement strategies when it just isn't possible to make everyone love you. Since every Influencer Snapshot® will be a little bit different from another, we encourage you to think creatively about what it will take to improve your situation or preserve it.

Building Advocacy

More selling happens at your customer's site when you are not there than when you are, which makes it really important to have the support of a vocal (and hopefully influential) advocate. How do we find advocates? They don't just drop from the sky, but they do grow on trees. Sort of. Salespeople have to plant and then nourish them carefully like they would a valuable plant. Here are some suggestions that have paid dividends:

- Present solutions that help them succeed in their jobs.
- Strive to be an asset which they can use to improve their image.

- Be a value-added resource who isn't always trying to sell them something, but rather who is trying to help them in as many ways possible.
- Don't "love 'em and leave 'em"; keep in constant contact with them to continually build the relationship.
- Ask them for help (after you've earned the right).
- Use other advocates to help you determine who else is likely to be helpful — someone who has authority within their organization (it isn't going to be all that helpful to have a key advocate that no one likes, respects or listens to).

Utilizing Your Advocates

Your greatest asset is a strongly influential advocate. These people can help you develop better movement strategies for improving your picture and planning your next steps. You can also use them to counteract your adversaries. Their influence makes them extremely important.

However, having influential advocates has at least two traps lying in wait. Our friend Mike fell into the trap of **over-relying** on his advocate to champion his solution to others inside the organization. He had put his sale into the hands of his advocate and hoped for the best, but as the wise man said, "Wishful thinking is not exactly a strategy."

The second trap ready to be sprung is **over-focusing** on the others in the organization because you believe your advocate is already sold. You may think, "Why bother preaching to the choir? She's already in our camp." This often leaves your strongest advocate open for the competition to sway her, which makes for a very nasty surprise come decision day. Remember, just because someone is your advocate doesn't mean they are not speaking with your competitor, and your competitor's strategy is to convert your advocates over to their solution. The moment you believe your competitors have stopped selling in your accounts is when you wake up surprised that the account is no longer yours.

Let's look at it from a different lens; let's say you are lucky enough to have a highly influential advocate. It does not mean you can ignore all of the other key influences involved in the decision process. On the contrary, it might be useful to pay even closer attention to them as you develop your plan. What do you do with the influencer who opposes you? Can they be turned? What about the advocate who has little influence? Are there ways you can help their voice be heard in the organization, thereby increasing their influence? It would be unusual to have someone whose influence cannot be increased. This is because the influence on a decision is not typically positional (that is, the title is not equivalent to the level of influence).

Helping your less-influential advocates understand the scope of the problem you are solving and its impact on the company, as well as quantifying the payoff of your proposed solution, can be crucial in gaining more influence. Do they understand the "pain and the gain"? Can they effectively communicate them to other decision influencers?

Also, how certain are you of your advocates' influence or their loyalty to you? Is there a risk that they may feel the same enthusiasm for your competitor's solution? Are they willing to "sell" your ideas to others?

Once you have become absolutely certain that an individual is your advocate and yours alone, then the question becomes: "What will they do to help you, by influencing others in the organization who are adversaries or are yet undecided?"

In Mike's case, his champion was truly his advocate. This individual had worked with Mike's company and knew the real value of their solutions. He had also been advocating for Mike's company before the real opportunity actually presented itself. And lastly, this person had proven to be supportive of Mike by arranging meetings and speaking to others on Mike's behalf. Mike now had to find additional ways to leverage his advocate's support.

Increasing/Decreasing Influence

Remember, when it comes to key influencers, your greatest asset is a *highly influential* advocate. While it is nice to have anyone on your side, they are far more helpful if they have influence over others. Can you make someone more influential? Can you alter the role someone will play in the decision-making process? Shock alert! The short answer to these questions is "YES!" Now, let us explain.

First, it is important to remember that a person's level of influence is determined by two factors: (1) their **ability** to influence others (role, credibility, persuasive skills, etc.) and (2) their **willingness** to influence others. One way to increase someone's influence is to promote them to a higher-level position in the organization where they have more influence by the nature of their title. Unfortunately, you don't usually have the power to grant that promotion. However, there are other ways of increasing a person's ability to influence others. Here are a couple of ideas:

- Arm them with the right information
- Practice key messaging points so their efforts to "sell" others are more successful
- Encourage them to share their opinions with others

Probably the biggest opportunity to grow someone's level of influence in a specific decision-making process is to appeal to their *willingness* to influence others. Many influencers simply sit on the sidelines holding their opinions because they want to look open-minded or objective about the decision. If you don't succeed in getting your advocates to be more influential, we can assure you that your competition will. In order to get your passive advocates to become engaged in the process, you have to motivate them by showing them why they need to engage. You have to highlight the impact an unfavorable decision is going to have on them and their position. A person doesn't have to be an executive or high-level employee to have influence over others. Sometimes passion is as important as position. Below are a few ideas you can consider to increase someone's Willingness to influence others:

- Highlight and quantify the impact the decision will have on them, both personally and professionally (i.e. longer work hours, more pay, impact on bonus, promotion/demotion, increase in stress, more detailed work, etc.).

- Provide support and opportunity for them to voice their opinions to others.

The last and trickiest part of developing a strategy to increase someone's level of influence is remembering that one person's influence is relative to the others involved. If you are going to move someone up the Influencer Snapshot's® "Influence Scale," then someone has to move down. This can be a great way to deal with Adversaries who have more relative influence. You can read more about that in the next segment. Just remember, just because you convince someone to be more vocal in a decision does not mean they automatically gain more influence. You have to arm them with the tools they need to truly influence others– not just make a lot of noise.

Dealing With Adversaries

Whenever we help a sales team create an Influencer Snapshot® and then ask them what they are going to do about their adversaries, the responses are often comical. First, there is silence, followed by the proposal of a diabolical plot to have the person's kneecaps broken in the parking lot!

We know these answers are in jest (or at least we hope so), but the first genuine reaction from almost everyone is befuddled confusion. Fortunately, there are approaches which experience has shown to be useful in counteracting and managing adversaries.

On the Influencer Snapshot®, there are three directions you could potentially move an adversary:

(1) To the Right by changing the way that person perceives you - make them less adversarial to your cause;
(2) Down by reducing that person's level of influence in the decision-making process; or,
(3) Down and to the Right - a combination of #1 and #2.

To determine which movement strategy (#1, #2 or #3) is going to be most appropriate and most successful, you first need to know why the individual is an adversary in the first place. Is it that they truly dislike you, your company, or your products? Or are they just more favorable toward a competitor? It is important to figure out if they are actively hostile toward you or simply in favor of your competitor.

We tend to view all adversaries as bad news, but some news is worse than others. The actively hostile adversary is, in some ways, much more dangerous than the passively opposed. On the other hand, we have seen actively hostile adversaries overplay their position and compromise their influence. And while passively opposed adversaries may not be as uncomfortable to us (we tend to attribute their opposition to simple ignorance), they are also often tough to persuade.

There is no one-size-fits-all approach to dealing with adversaries. Your strategies and tactics have to take into account many factors, among them the adversaries' levels of influence and their degree of hostility.

In our friend Mike's situation, he was facing two types of adversaries, and they required different types of approaches. The first adversary was someone who presented a significant roadblock to Mike and his sales efforts. In fact, Mike referred to her as a "dust-storm." This individual had been responsible for implementing the existing technology and viewed any outside upgrade solutions as a threat to her own legacy. She knew very little about Mike's company or its capabilities but had still managed to plant significant doubt over Mike's solutions among the decision team. On the one hand, she was a storm that people were aware of and she created an impact that shouldn't be ignored. On the other hand, she did not seem to have an extraordinary level of influence, even though she was stirring up a lot of dust and making a lot of noise.

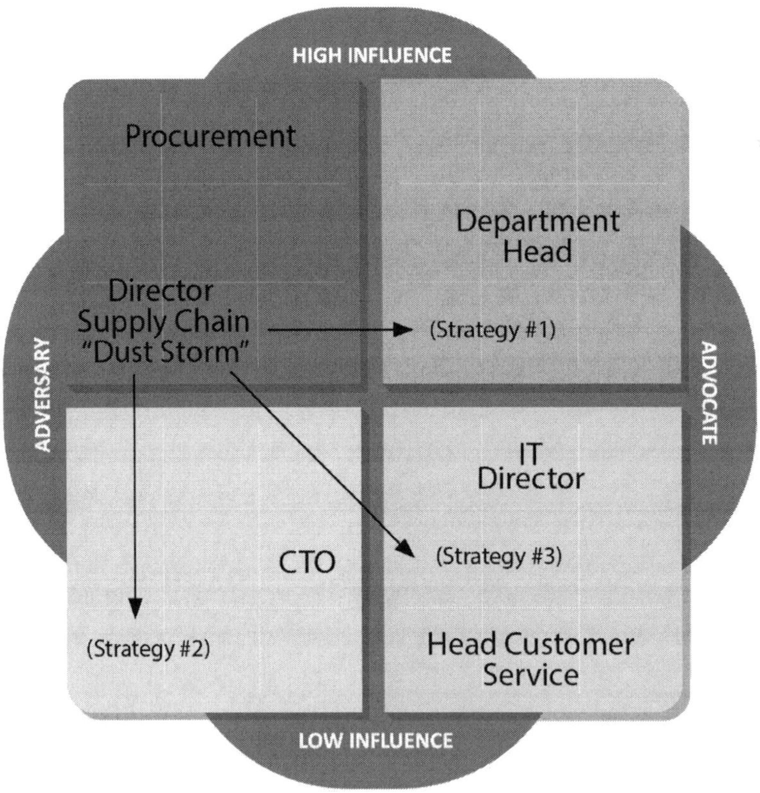

The second adversary in Mike's situation was, interestingly enough, more powerful than the first. This individual was skeptical of Mike's products but didn't have any allegiance to Mike's competitors. She was highly influential, but only moderately adversarial. It was clear that Mike recognized that he had two people in the organization that weren't supporters of his solutions.

Unfortunately, Mike's approach to managing these two adversaries is all too frequently found with many of the salespeople we work with in the field. Mike's strategy to manage his "dust-storm" adversary was to just let her continue to try and create chaos, but not worry too much about it because he felt that her influence didn't carry much weight. Mike's big mistake was assuming that low influence meant no influence. This happens all too often when developing a plan to manage the key influencers involved in a decision. If you have identified and validated the top five or six key influencers in a decision, you can't afford to ignore any of them. They have been selected to provide their input in the decision process, therefore, they shouldn't be ignored. Mike's second mistake was not building a proactive strategy to manage his "skeptic." Remember, this person had a high influence on the decision but was only considered to be a moderate adversary. As Mike told us, he simply viewed his "skeptic" as not having loyalty to his company or the competitors. Unfortunately for Mike, his competitors saw this individual influencer in the same light but elected to take action and strengthen their position with her. His competitor was able to turn this person that didn't seem to care either way about what solution the company elected to invest in and turn them into their advocate. The lesson learned for Mike was even though he completed his Influencer Snapshot® he never took the time to share it with his manager or any of his peers. If he would have shared his picture and movement strategy with others, they might have exposed to him the importance of doing anything you can to take high-level influencers and strengthen their advocacy towards your solution, even if it's just enough to tip the scale in your favor.

In Susan's case, she was proactive in asking questions to quickly determine who the key influencers were in her customer's decision process and what their opinion was towards Susan's software solution compared to the competition. Susan mapped out her Influencer Snapshot®, created two key movement strategies, one to strengthen a moderate advocate and another to attempt to neutralize a high influence adversary. Susan recognized that she might be overlooking something and wanted to test her assumptions with her manager, so they sat down to examine and dissect the preliminary movement strategies. Much to Susan's surprise, she walked away from meeting with her managers with two alternative strategies. Her manager asked a number of questions that challenged her strategic thinking and tested her assumptions. As a result, Susan executed her movement strategy and was able to quickly neutralize her high-influence adversary. Developing a sales strategy isn't a one-person job. It's always better to bounce ideas and alternatives off of a manager or peer. They are often more objective since they are not as close to the account.

Regardless of why someone is an adversary, **the goal is to make this person either less opposed to you or less influential in the decision-making process.**

The challenge is in making that happen. This is why a complete assessment of the key influencers within a buying opportunity is critical. Your Influencer Snapshot® is what helps you determine the best course of action.

Chapter 4 Summary

In this chapter, we explained the three steps to building an Influencer Snapshot® for your sales opportunities:

The three steps are:

1. Identify *all* the key players who may exert influence in the decision-making process.
2. Determine how each key influencer feels about you - are they an advocate or an adversary?
3. Gauge the influence of each key influencer involved in the buying process.

Getting to know your key influencers is incredibly crucial to building a successful Influencer Snapshot®. Who are they? What do they want? Why do they want it? You do not have to be omniscient or omnipotent. You just have to invest the time and ask the right questions.

As you've seen with Mike and Susan throughout the chapter, it's crucial to have an understanding of who your key influencers are so you can build an accurate Influencer Snapshot®. Susan was able to successfully close and win the sale because she asked the right questions to learn the identities of everyone that would be influential during the decision-making process and used that information to her advantage. In addition, Susan tested her strategies with her manager and discovered an alternative approach that ended up helping Susan win the business. Mike, on the other hand, made the dangerous assumption that the key influencers who'd been involved in previous decisions would once again be the key to his success. Mike failed to ask the right questions and his assumptions ultimately lost him the sale.

Remember, as you add layers to your picture by populating the Influencer Snapshot®, some influencers' positions may change over time. Someone who is adversarial toward you today may warm up to you over time. Someone who lacks influence now may become more influential in the future.

The whole idea of building the Influencer Snapshot® is to get a visual of your position and figure out ways to **strengthen your position.** This tool can help you in your efforts to identify and execute strategies to develop influential advocates and overcome influential adversaries.

Chapter Questions

These questions are designed to engage you in understanding how to manage key influencers inside your opportunities. Like in the previous chapter, think of a current sales opportunity you are working on, and ask yourself these questions:

1. With which influencer do you believe you have the greatest opportunity to increase their level of advocacy for your solution? What are two things you can do to increase that person's level of Advocacy for your solution?

2. Which advocate can you best leverage to help you neutralize one of your adversaries? What steps do you need to take to ensure this advocate is willing and able to help you?

3. If your competition completed an Influencer Snapshot® who would be on their Influencer Snapshot® tool that is not on yours? What can you do about it?

4. What is one way to reduce the level of influence of a high influence adversary

This book helps validate why price is rarely the key that locks in the deal. If it is…it's a race to the bottom! Truly uncovering and aligning to our Customer's Decision Criteria is integral to success.

Shane Robinson
Global Sales Trainer
Abbott

Chapter 5

Influencing the Competitive Landscape

Throughout the past 20 years, we have worked with salespeople with varying levels of experience across a broad spectrum of industries. In our work with these clients, we've evaluated sales opportunities that were both won and lost. When we've asked salespeople to explain the reason they lost an opportunity, a common culprit frequently rears its ugly head—price.

It is easy to blame Price for a lost sale, and sometimes it really is the culprit. But frequently it isn't. In fact, our research has shown that 86 percent of salespeople interviewed said that price was the number one reason a buying decision went in favor of their competitor. Yet, after we conducted a loss analysis with those customers, we found that in only 19 percent of the cases, the customer selected the low-cost provider. It is important to note that "Price" didn't always mean the competitor had a lower purchasing price for the product or solution. In some cases, "price" was defined as a bundled solution or better financing options. But the important takeaway is that salespeople are NOT losing to "Price" as often as they think.

While working with Mike and Susan's company, the Chief Revenue Officer shared with us that salespeople inside the company were constantly complaining to management about losing deals because of price. Senior management believed the current pricing model was appropriate. But, to be sure, they needed a deeper analysis with real feedback from lost prospects and new customers.

So, the leadership team asked us to interview some new customers (wins) and a number of prospects and former customers that had elected made a shift to work with the competition (losses). In these interviews, the first thing we explored was the decision criteria these companies used to evaluate our customer's solutions against the other solutions being considered. Although the definitions used by the prospects to describe their decision criteria weren't always the same, the most common criteria mentioned were data security, supplier innovation, software compatibility, ease of use and price.

We then asked the prospects to rank their top three most important criteria. Surprisingly, the price was only in the top three for only 15 percent of those surveyed. Instead, the majority of those surveyed put in their top three Data Security, Portability of the software and SaaS Integration. One customer was even quoted as saying, "If the product couldn't interface with our existing system, then our staff wouldn't use it and productivity wouldn't improve."

One of the clients we interviewed was an account that had been managed by Mike for nearly seven years. According to Mike, the client had elected to end the seven-year relationship because the competition had a lower acquisition price. It's difficult to lose a long-term customer. It's even more difficult to lose when you feel your company doesn't support you by being willing to give up a few margin points to keep a great customer. Needless to say, Mike was not happy about this loss. Before interviewing his customer, we interviewed Mike, asking three simple questions. The interview went something like this:

> **Ignite Selling:** *Other than "price", what were the other three or four criteria this customer was using to compare your solution to the competition?*
>
> **Mike's Response**: *The most important criteria was the price, but the other criteria were probably Support, Service and experience in the market.*
>
> **Ignite Selling**: *How did the customer rank these decision criteria from most essential to least essential?*

Mike's Response: *As I said, "Price" was the most important criteria, followed by Service, Market Experience, and then Support.*

Ignite Selling: *Who's decision criteria and ranking did this belong to?*

Mike's Response: *Umm… this decision criterion came from Chris, the Director of IT. She was driving the decision.*

We weren't trying to embarrass Mike; we were simply trying to gain some critical insights before we went to interview his customer. Mike then arranged a time for us to meet Chris, the Director of IT and his strongest advocate in the account, so we could interview her for our analysis.

In our interview, we asked Chris a similar set of questions. Please see the questions and responses below:

Ignite Selling: *Chris, what were the top four decision criteria you used to compare Mike's company to the solution provider you selected?*

Customer's Response: *I'd say my top four decision criteria were Data Security, Reporting Capabilities, SaaS integration and Pricing*

Ignite Selling: *If you had to rank these criteria from most essential to least essential, what would that look like?*

Customer's Response: *We'll that's pretty easy for me, it would be the following: Reporting Capabilities, Data Security, Price and Saas Integration.*

Ignite Selling: *How well was Mike's company able to meet your expectations with those criteria compared to the competition?*

Customer's Response: *For the most part, they were very compatible, both companies are excellent in what they provide. The main reason I recommended we go with Mike's competitor was that I liked their reporting capabilities better. I didn't think Mike's system provided us with the reporting capabilities that would help us improve productivity. With our new partner, my team doesn't have to spend nearly as much time dissecting data.*

Ignite Selling: *Other than yourself, who else played a major role in this decision?*

Customer's Response: *There were four of us that had input into the decision, but the top two key decision-makers were Paul, our CTO and Margaret our CFO.*

We continued our analysis by interviewing the CTO and CFO to get their answers to the same questions we just asked Chris. For the most part, the responses were very similar. The only difference was that the CTO had ranked "Software Portability" as his number-one criteria.

When we took the interview responses back to Mike and his management team, they were surprised. Even more, they were disappointed. Mike initially had a hard time accepting the data we shared with him, which isn't surprising. Most salespeople struggle with losing. This is what makes them great at what they do. It took some time for Mike to digest the responses from his customer. It also forced him to examine the possible assumptions he made throughout the sales process.

What really upset Mike, in the end, is that Chris' number one criteria was "Reporting Capabilities" not "Price"; and even more disappointing is that Mike never once talked about reporting capabilities because he assumed it wasn't overly important in Chris' decision and he thought his solution was just as good, if not better than his competitor's.

Unfortunately, this is a common scenario. Many salespeople don't know the decision criteria their customers are using to compare them to the competition, much less which criterion is most important to the customer. Salespeople also assume, often incorrectly, that they are working with the *one* person most likely to help them close the opportunity and assume that his/her criteria are the same as everyone else in the organization.

What's Your Competitive Position?

How do you compare with your competitors in the eyes of your customer? This is your **competitive position**. The tool we use to visualize your competitive position is called the Competitive Snapshot®. Use the four steps described below to complete an accurate Competitive Snapshot®:

Step #1 – Identifying Decision Criteria

Competitive analysis isn't complicated, even when there are a large number of competitors in the mix. Customers typically make buying decisions following a reasonably predictable pattern.

First, customers evaluate what's important and determine what **decision criteria** they will use to assess alternatives. Second, they determine what alternative options they want to consider and then evaluate those options against the decision criteria they determined in Step 1. And lastly, they select the option that best aligns with their priorities. This is a reasonable approach to decision-making, and regardless of how we might perceive them, in this regard prospects are predictable.

Let me give you a real-life example around an important decision my wife, Sherry, and I had to make recently. A few years ago, we moved from Clifton, Virginia to the small town of Dripping Springs, Texas. As you can imagine, moving halfway across the country provided us with a lot of important decisions to make. We had to decide which town to live in, what type of house we wanted to move into, which church we would go to, and many others. In every decision, consciously and unconsciously, we had a set of criteria that were important to both of us. When it came to choosing a church for us to attend, our natural decision was to go find a Lutheran Church similar to what we had experienced in Virginia. Unfortunately, there were no similar churches within a 30-minute drive from our new home. Therefore, Sherry and I consciously created a list of decision criteria for what we wanted in our next church. Our decision criteria were the following:

- Did the pastor preach to us in a meaningful way? Did they speak to our lives?
- Did the church have a worship band? (I played guitar in our band in Virginia and it became an important part of worship for Sherry and me.)
- Were there elements of a traditional liturgy? Readings, prayers, communion, etc.
- Was the church growing in membership or was it beginning to decline?

Sherry and I were very intentional in our search for a new church. We started with our online research, reading websites and watching recorded sermons. We visited a few local churches that we found online and began talking with people attending these churches. When talking with these church members, we would ask them to speak to the criteria we'd developed. This process not only allowed us to find our ideal church but also enabled us to make the decision quickly.

Your customers go through a similar process to determine what's important to them and what is incidental. As a salesperson, when it comes to competitive analysis, **Our first task is to uncover our customer's decision criteria.**

Step #2 – Adding Decision Criteria

After compiling a list of decision criteria your customer will use to assess you against the competition, it makes sense to consider whether there are any criteria the customer hasn't considered but should consider.

Your goal is to help the customer make the most informed decision possible. Are there other decision criteria your customer should consider that would help make them make a more informed decision? If so, you want to convince your customer to add those criteria to their list.

So, what criteria should you add? Let's go back to the example of Sherry and I looking for a new church. You read that we initially had four key decision criteria that we felt were important to us. Using only these criteria, we had narrowed our options down to two churches. However, we could only select one of them as our future church home. In one of our conversations with the leaders of Dripping Springs Presbyterian Church, the conversation turned to our interest in supporting local community outreach. Although this was something Sherry and I enjoyed doing a lot with our church back in Virginia, it was not something Sherry and I had put on our initial decision criteria list. By checking our interest and by highlighting the work the church's Mission Team does with local and regional community outreach, the leaders, Pastor Nancy and Pastor Mitch, helped set Dripping Springs Presbyterian Church apart from the competition, and ultimately helped us make the decision to join their congregation. Now, the other church might have been doing some great community outreach as well. But, because these two pastors took the initiative to bring it up in our conversations, they differentiated themselves in our eyes. When you bring additional decision criteria to the conversation that you believe the customer should be considering, it not only helps the customer make a better decision, it also serves to quickly set you apart from the competition.

Step #3 – Ranking the Importance of Decision Criteria

After compiling a comprehensive list of decision criteria, the next task is to get the customer to rank the decision in order of importance, from most important to least. As you can imagine, the scale of importance is relative. Each criterion is ranked relative to the others. And keep in mind, not only may each influencer have their own decision criteria, they may also assess the importance of the decision criteria differently.

Let's return to our church example one more time. Sherry and I started the process by asking ourselves "What's most important to us in a new church? What is essential to us and what is "nice to have?" While a salesperson might use a number of different questions to uncover and explore decision criteria, the desired outcome is insight into what's important to your customer.

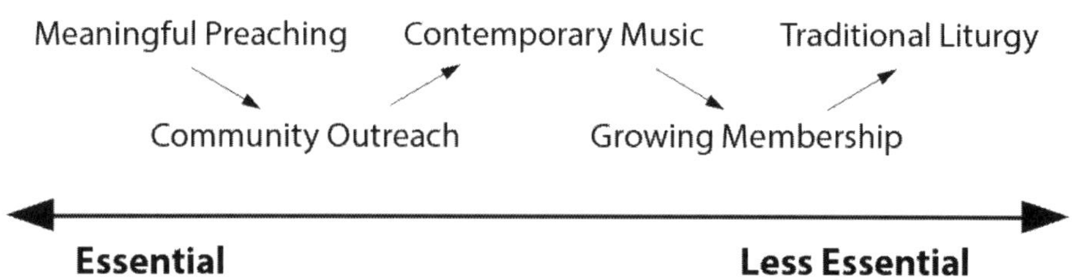

Inevitably, identifying a customer's decision criteria highlights conflict between competing "desires." In our church example, we might have initially said that great preaching is as important as great worship music. If both decision criteria are considered equally important, how do you break the tie? How do you rank criteria relative to each other? They must have a relative ranking. Even if a customer states that several criteria are "equally important," they may ultimately have to choose between them.

For many salespeople, (and for people in general), this is a difficult task. The question here is: "What are you willing to sacrifice?" Just asking the question highlights the possibility that the customer might not be able to get everything they want, which can certainly create disappointment.

Let's see how Susan successfully applied the concept of validating how a customer assesses the importance of various decision criteria. Susan had recently closed a new opportunity with a single division of a large, contract manufacturing company. After a successful implementation of her inventory management software solution, Susan hoped to use the momentum she'd gained with that division to springboard to other divisions inside the account. When another opportunity arose inside the account just three months later, it appeared that Susan was well positioned. The company was familiar with Susan's solution, they understood her pricing module, and she had a successful track record to fall back on.

Although there were a few new influencers involved in the decision-making process for this new opportunity, some of the same individuals who were involved in the last decision (that Susan won) were also going to be involved in this decision. When asked, one of those key influencers told Susan that the decision criteria for this decision would pretty much mirror the decision criteria used in the last decision. Most salespeople would have accepted that answer and moved on to implement their strategy. But Susan took a different approach. Susan knew there was a new competitor in the mix.

After doing some digging, Susan learned that the competitive sales representatives had been spending a great deal of time emphasizing reporting capabilities in meetings with the CTO and the Director of this other division. In their efforts, the competition had done a nice job raising the level of importance of "reporting capabilities" in the eyes of the customer. SaaS Integration, which had been the most important decision criteria in the last decision, was no longer the most important decision criteria for the customer. Not only had Susan's competitor raised the importance of reporting capabilities, but they had also convinced the CTO that their capabilities were far superior to that of Susan's company.

Susan thought her company's reporting capabilities were just as good, if not better than those of her competitor. To succeed, Susan would need to somehow convince the CTO that her reporting capabilities did indeed match up. If Susan couldn't make that happen, then her alternative was to change the prospect's perception on what's important – which means convincing the CTO and others that "reporting capabilities" aren't as important as SaaS Integration, Portability and Data Security.

Step #4 – Understanding the Customer's Perception of Us

Discovering and ranking selection criteria is only a part of your job when it comes to the competitive analysis process. You must also understand the competitive advantages and disadvantages of your solution, which requires gaining insight into how the customer believes your solutions stack up against the competition. What's important is that you gain the *customer's perspective* of your capabilities. We already have an opinion about how our capabilities match up, but our opinions don't matter.

Several years ago, Kevin and his wife relocated from their home in the Washington, DC area. When they were evaluating their geographic options, one of their major selection criteria was the weather.

Kevin thought, "My wife does not like heat and humidity, which rules out portions of the Southeast and Southwest. And I don't like places that experience snowfall any later than February, which eliminates much of the Northeast and parts of the central plains." So, out of their shortlist of cities, they selected Portland, Oregon, which is very well known for having abundant cloud coverage and lots of rain.

When Kevin explains to people how they made their decision and mentions that Portland had a relative position of strength with regard to weather, people look at him with surprise. How does Portland win with the weather? Well, it's all in how you define good weather.

A customer's perception of which competitive alternative does best with a specific decision criterion reminds us of the proverbs: "Beauty is in the eye of the beholder" or, "One person's trash is another person's treasure." A salesperson might firmly believe he has a competitive advantage with a specific criterion, but his opinion matters little. It's what the customer believes that's important. We must look at the decision criteria through the customer's eyes. Doing this will reveal how we must improve our competitive position. Like in the situation we just spoke about with Susan, the CTO was convinced that Susan's competitor had better "reporting capabilities" and that those capabilities were more important than any other decision criteria. Whether Susan agreed with the CTO or not, it was the perception of her customer.

In Susan's case, this meant assessing the perspective of her key influencers, primarily the CTO. Did their perspectives match up with Susan's own perspective on her areas of strength and weakness? In this most recent win/loss analysis, if Susan wouldn't have met with the CTO, he likely would have made the decision to partner with her competitor.

Getting your customer to describe honestly how you stack up to their decision criteria can be challenging for a couple of reasons. First, some customers may be reluctant to tell the truth because they do not want to risk offending you. A second reason may be that they do not want to give you any negotiating leverage. A third reason can be that they do not want to tilt the competitive playing field by revealing too much about who's in front and who's not.

One strategy we have seen top sellers use to gain insights into the mind of the customer is to rely on key advocates. They are already ostensibly in your corner, and, if you've done your job well in cultivating them and helping them improve their influence, they can provide invaluable information.

Your customer will prioritize certain decision criteria based on what is essential to them choosing a solution. So, whether you think you have a comparative advantage, it's ultimately up to your customer. Candid, detailed feedback from your customer can help you align your solution to your customer's needs.

The more insight you can get about how your customer evaluates their options, the more accurate your assessment will be.

If you're unable to learn firsthand how the customer sees things, then you will have to rely upon careful guesswork. What's your customer's buying history? How does the market perceive you and your competitors? What have other customers said about you? While this method is certainly more analytical than fortune-telling, it may prove in the end to be no more reliable. How unbiased can you be? Who else on your team can provide a balanced perspective on the situation?

Outlining the Strategy

These four steps described above are the steps required to build an accurate and complete Competitive Snapshot®. When complete, it will help you emphasize your Strengths, minimize your Weaknesses, exploit your Opportunities and neutralize your Threats.

The vertical axis on the Competitive Snapshot® shows how essential the decision criteria is to the customer, while the horizontal axis represents how your customer perceives your ability to support their criteria as compared to your competition.

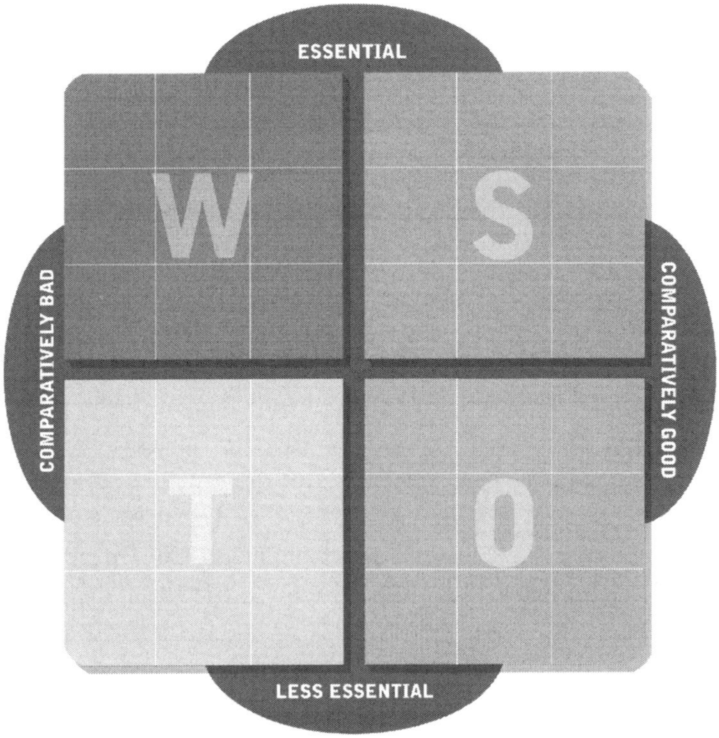

The Competitive Snapshot's® two-by-two matrix helps salespeople do one thing: **Better manage the decision criteria the customer is using to compare them against the competition.** To complete the Snapshot®, you have to answer the four familiar questions below:

1. **What are the decision criteria?** Identify the criteria your customer is using to compare you against the competition.

2. **What decision criteria are missing**? What criteria should you be adding?

3. **How does the customer rank those criteria?** What does your customer perceive as the most essential criteria to least essential?

4. **How does that customer perceive the competition?** Are you comparatively a good option or a bad option?

The goal of using a tool such as this is to develop a clear, visual picture of how your offering compares to your competitors. The tool can be used regardless of the number of competitors—or the types of competition—confronting you because it focuses on decision criteria and your relative position of strength for each of those criteria.

Let's look at Susan's situation and use this tool to evaluate her competitive position.

Accurately completing this tool is a little more challenging than completing some of the other tools introduced thus far, simply because you have to get inside your customer's head to assess the situation accurately. In addition, the Competitive Snapshot® illustrates your competitive position from only *one influencer's perspective.*

Every key influencer involved in a purchasing decision will have their own unique perspective on the decision criteria that should be used to assess competitive alternatives. However, this doesn't mean you necessarily need to do a competitive analysis for everyone who might have influence in the decision-making process. Like we emphasized in the Influencer Snapshot® chapter, focus your strategic planning efforts on the three or four people who will have the most influence over the decision. Identify those individuals, find out what their decision criteria are and how they rank those criteria.

All that being said, simply putting words onto the tool is only the beginning of your competitive strategy. It's what you do with this information that matters.

A Picture Is Worth a Thousand Words

When complete, the Competitive Snapshot® puts the customer's Decision Criteria into one of four buckets based on how important the decision criteria are to the customer, and how the customer believes you stack up against the competition. The four buckets are described below:

Strengths: In our Competitive Snapshot® tool, *Strengths* are those decision criteria considered to be essential by your customer and in which the customer believes you are better than the competing alternatives. The Movement Strategies we'll discuss later in this chapter don't directly address Strengths because we don't want to "move" Strengths – we want to keep them right where they are. As a result, Sellers often become complacent about their Strengths by acting as though a customer's opinion of them will not shift or change over time.

One approach salespeople often take when it comes to dealing with Strengths is to continuously emphasize how good their capabilities are compared to the alternatives. Most salespeople default to this approach because they are comfortable touting what they are good at. Who is not?

Getting the customer to articulate why the decision criterion is important in the first place is a more impactful way of dealing with Strengths. The first, and perhaps most important reason, has to do with an old selling proverb: "If you say it, they can doubt it; but if they say it, it's true." The second reason has to do with ownership. When the customer expresses their rationale behind rating a decision criterion as "essential," they specify why they want what they want in their own words. They own it, therefore they are then better able to communicate the rationale to others (to defend it, in other words).

The most important thing to remember is that you need your prospects to want what it is you're good at. Getting the customer to tell you why the decision criterion that you happen to be good is important to them is one way to accomplish that objective.

Weakness: In our Competitive Snapshot® tool, the decision criteria that your customer sees as important but where you are at a comparative disadvantage to your competition are considered weaknesses. For instance, if a customer regards reputation as *very important*, but believes your company doesn't have a good reputation when compared to the alternatives, it would be a weakness. The challenge in dealing with weakness is that it's difficult to make a customer care less about something that they feel strongly about. (Have you ever tried to persuade someone on the opposite side of the political aisle to care less about their favorite issues? How did that go?)

Opportunity: In our Competitive Snapshot® tool, we have an opportunity when there is a Decision Criterion in which the customer believes that we are strong but unfortunately doesn't care very much about it. Opportunities have the potential to become Strengths if the seller can make that criterion more important in the eyes of the customer. For example, let's say that customer service is one of your customer's decision criteria, but it's less important than three other key criteria. And this customer believes you are very good at providing outstanding customer service. Your strategy might be to find a way to make this decision criteria more important or essential in the mind of your customer. In other words, increase the importance of the criteria that the customer believes you are comparatively good.

Threats: In the Competitive Snapshot® tool, Threats are merely the opposite side of Opportunities. A Decision Criteria that is a Threat is something the customer doesn't care as much about, which is a good thing, because they don't think we are very good at it. One common mistake we see salespeople make when confronted with the threat is to ignore it, ostrich-style. Maybe if we do not bring it up, they seem to think, it will go away of its own accord. This approach has its temptations. After all, if it's not important to the customer, why bring it up? Let sleeping dogs lie. Unfortunately, if you don't bring it up, who will? Well, obviously, the competition will.

It's important to consider the four quadrants in the Competitive Snapshot®– Strengths, Weaknesses, Opportunities and Threats– so that you can look quickly at the Snapshot® to determine what action you need to take first.

Let's return to our friend Susan. In her situation, the Competitive Snapshot® showed there were two Strengths: SaaS Integration capabilities and the Portability of the System. These attributes were essential to this customer, and the customer believed that Susan's solution was better than the competition.

According to the Snapshot®, there was only one Weakness, and it was a big one. Reporting Capabilities was ranked as the most important decision criteria to the customer and was an area in which the customer felt that Susan's solution was comparatively bad. Even though Susan's price was higher than that of her competitors, the customer didn't seem to think it was as important as other criteria, so it was categorized as a threat. The final decision criterion was Data Security. Even though Susan's solution was comparatively good with Data Security, the customer didn't care very much, thus making it an Opportunity.

Once you have drawn the picture and determined where the decision criteria fall, you can better determine what kind of strategic actions need to be taken to improve your competitive position. To help, let's look at three movement strategies that can help alter a Competitive Snapshot® in your favor.

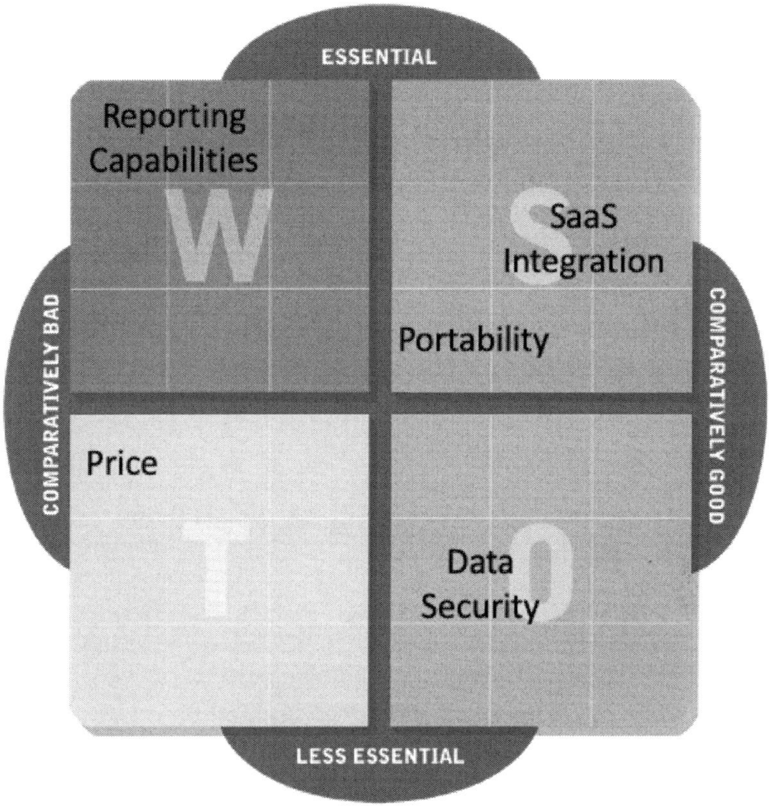

Improve

The **Improve** Movement Strategy is all about changing the perception the customer has of your capabilities and how you stack up against the competition. If a customer believes you are Comparatively Bad with a specific decision criteria, then you want to change that perception. The first question to answer is: "Is the customer correct?" Are we really Comparatively Bad at that decision criteria, or is it just a misperception?" In either case, you have to PROVE to the customer that you are better than he/she thinks you are or demonstrate that you are taking appropriate steps to address your performance issues.

It's not uncommon for a customer to perceive your competitor's product as stronger in certain areas, but we can't just tell the customer they're wrong. We need to be smart. This is where the **Improve** Movement Strategy can help. Once Susan recognized that the CTO perceived her "reporting capabilities" to be inferior to that of the competition, there were several things she tried. First, Susan asked questions to understand why the negative perception existed and then developed a strategy to change that perception. Second, Susan used references to provide evidence that her solution's reporting capabilities were better than the CTO believed. And finally, Susan conducted a demonstration showing exactly how her system could help improve the productivity of the team, thus using the old adage, "evidence defeats doubt." There were probably more actions Susan could have taken to change the customer's perception of her reporting capabilities, but these three steps helped narrow the performance gap enough to make "reporting capabilities" a non-issue.

Remember, the **Improve** Movement Strategy is all about improving the perception that the customer has around one or more of their decision criteria where they believe you are Comparatively Bad.

Redefine

This movement strategy is all about changing the way a customer defines a decision criterion. The Redefine Strategy is implemented by either broadening or narrowing the definition of the decision criterion so the customer sees you in a more favorable light. The Redefine Movement Strategy can be implemented on any decision criterion, even if it has already been clearly defined by the customer. Redefining is an attempt by the seller to change the way the customer defines the criteria so that it puts the seller's solution in a more favorable light.

This strategy can be used when dealing with any decision criteria on the Competitive Snapshot®, but it is most often used to address decision criteria the customer views as essential and where the customer perceives your solution (as they've defined it) to be comparatively weak against the competition.

Let's consider a common example where a redefining movement strategy can be applied - Price. In Susan's case, Price ranked four out of five in terms of importance. However, Susan's solution was considerably more expensive when compared to her competition – thus making Price a *Threat* on the Competitive Snapshot® tool. Most of the companies we work with sell a premium solution with a premium price tag – they are *not* the low-cost provider in their market. There is no shame in selling a premium priced solution. In fact, having a solution to sell that has more to offer than just a low price creates a wonderful opportunity for salespeople to be successful if they have confidence in the value their product brings and the skills to translate that value into something meaningful to the customer. No one should be ashamed or frustrated to be the premium-priced solution in their market.

Most of what's been written about overcoming "price" objections emphasize the need to create more value to justify the higher price. We don't disagree with this common notion. In fact, in the next chapter, we're going to introduce you to our ***Value* Snapshot**® tool which is designed to help you better align your unique differentiators to the business metrics of your customer. However, there are more strategies you can implement when a customer says, "Getting the best price is important to me, and your solution is more expensive than the competition." The easiest, but less attractive movement strategy to overcome Price is to **Improve** your position by simply discounting your solution. But, when it comes to Price, the **Improve** Movement Strategy shouldn't be your first plan of attack.

Like many other decision criteria, the definition of Price is open for interpretation. Price could be defined as the licensing fee or initial price tag. Price could include add-on services, such as professional service support or training fees. It could also include the other factors that may come along during an install, such as downtime, learning curve, etc. When applied to Price, the **Redefine** Movement Strategy is intended to change the definition of price to put you in a more favorable light. When we introduced this idea to Susan, she quickly came up with two ways she could have redefined "Price." One approach could have been to break down the total investment separating hardware, software and professional services to find out specifically where her price was higher than that of her competition. Susan then thought she could expand the value of those areas where her price was higher. In our planning, Susan said that her company's professional services fees are typically what drives the overall cost of their solution. Breaking it down and **Redefining** Price by the separate components helped her customer understand what made Susan's solution different and how their money was actually being spent. It also helped identify gaps in the competitor's solution that they wouldn't have seen otherwise.

Elevate

Elevate is a movement strategy designed to help a customer understand the importance of meeting a specific decision criterion. This specific strategy is used to make decision criteria more Essential in the eyes of the customer, thus often turning an Opportunity into a Strength.

Susan's customer believed that Data Security was important enough to include as a factor in their decision, but it was the least important of all the decision criteria. The customer also recognized that Susan's solution had a much better Data Security plan than her competitor. What could Susan do to **elevate** the importance of Data Security in the eyes of her customer? For one, Susan could have further explored the importance of Data Security and gotten the customer to consider the downside risks of not having effective Data Security in his system. By making the customer more aware of the consequences they would encounter if they didn't get the criterion met, she could have **Elevated** its importance in the eyes of the customer. Another idea that Susan implemented is to align the value that Data Security brought to the company goals for the upcoming year. She could have demonstrated how her company can better support her customer's business metrics through heightened Data Security, thus **Elevating** the importance of Data Security over more important decision criteria.

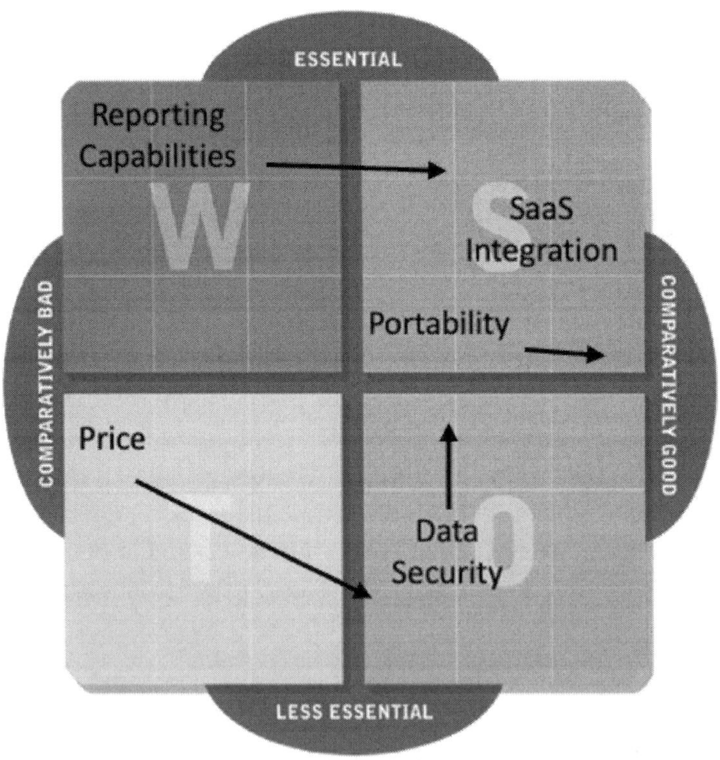

What Is Competition?

When we introduce the idea of competitive analysis to our clients, most begin the discussion with the Webster's Dictionary definition in mind: "The effort of two or more parties acting independently to secure the business of a third party by offering the most favorable terms."

Salespeople think only of their traditional, familiar competitors; ones who play in the same sandbox and sell similar solutions. What we find is that most of them tend to ignore non-traditional forms of competition.

Consequently, when we discuss competitive analysis with our clients, the first task before us is to remove their blinders and get them to look beyond the "traditional" competitors. Every alternative before their customer should be considered a legitimate competitor, and a well-thought-out competitive analysis needs to reflect the breadth of choices the customer has before them.

So, when you build a Competitive Snapshot® for your opportunities, be sure to broaden the definition of competition to include not just the traditional competitors, but also seemingly insignificant competitors and other competing internal projects. The process for building the Competitive Snapshot® with these new ads is the same, but the picture you will get as a result will be far more complete.

Chapter 5 Summary

In this chapter, we introduced you to the Competitive Snapshot®, which is a tool to help visualize and manage your competitor and your competitive position within a sales opportunity.

To build a complete and accurate Competitive Snapshot® involves four steps:

1. Identify the decision criteria your customer is using to compare you against the competition.

2. Add additional decision criteria you believe the customer has not considered, typically those items that differentiate you from your competitors.

3. Work with the customer to rank the decision criteria from Most Essential to Least Essential.

4. Confirm with your customer whether they perceive your ability to meet their decision criteria as Comparatively Good or Comparative Bad when compared to the competition.

Being able to execute these four simple factors can make the difference between you winning or losing an opportunity. Eighty-Six percent of salespeople blame "Price" as the reason they lost their last sale, yet when we conducted a "win-loss" analysis the truth is they lost to a lower-cost competitor 19 percent of the time. It's easy to blame "Price" when you don't know the other decision criteria the customer is using to compare your solution against the competition.

Chapter Questions

These questions are designed to engage you in understanding how to better manage the decision criteria your customers are using to compare you against your competition. Like in the previous chapters, think of a current sales opportunity you are working on, and ask yourself these questions:

1. What is your customer's decision criteria and how do they rank it from Most Essential to Less Essential?

2. Which one of your solution's unique differentiators is NOT listed in your customer's list of decision criteria? What can you do to get them to add this to the list?

3. Which decision criteria does the customer believe you are Comparative Bad and which Movement Strategy do you believe might help change this customer perspective?

4. Which decision criteria do you believe the customer is under-estimating and thus needs to be "Elevated" and made more important to this customer? What is your strategy to Elevate these Less Essential decision criteria?

I first met Steve Gielda over 25 years ago and saw him present at a Huthwaite National Sales Meeting. My first thought was, WOW, this guy is a masterful salesperson. Now Steve and Kevin have captured their years of experience helping other sales professionals excel. As they suggest at the end of Chapter 6, you can choose to ignore these proven concepts at your peril. Apply them and watch your win rates and commissions increase.

John Hoskins
Founder/Author
Level Five Selling

Chapter 6

Assessing the Value of Your Solution

Sales training programs focusing on "Consultative Selling Skills" have been around since the mid-1980s – if not longer. Since the advent of consultative selling skills, salespeople have been taught that to maximize value, a salesperson needs to show a tight connection between the features and benefits of his/her product and the stated needs of the customer. In addition to demonstrating solutions in a way that connects with needs, salespeople have been told to try to quantify the impact their solutions can have as a way of building a sound justification for the price or investment in their solution.

In 2012, we wrote our first book, *Premeditated Selling*. In that book, we introduced a tool called the Value Snapshot® that aligned our definition of value to the one described above, and even used a concept called the Value Equation (*Value = Benefits – Cost)* as a tool to help salespeople assess their value position for a given opportunity. The idea that a customer will purchase a solution if that solution has a positive Value Equation is persuasive. Think about it. Spending $10K for a solution that will bring $20K in benefits seems like a no-brainer. At the time, we believed that, when communicated properly, a positive Value Equation would be such a compelling argument that a salesperson could hardly lose.

And, we weren't alone. Several of the companies we've worked with over the years have actually employed a corporate sponsored "Value Calculator." A Value Calculator is a tool that can help salespeople demonstrate to the customer the economic impact their solutions can have by "calculating" the value in monetary terms. For example, one company we've worked with sells a medical device into operating rooms inside hospitals. This company's Value Calculator could calculate the amount of time their device could save per-procedure and ultimately convert that initial element of time into dollar savings, by including people cost, equipment cost, additional procedures, etc. The idea is to create a compelling economic story that would ultimately justify the investment in a higher-priced solution.

Unfortunately, evidence suggests that being able to demonstrate just a positive Value Equation isn't enough. In the win/loss analysis we described earlier in the book, we also asked questions about quantifiable Value and the impact it had on the customer's decision. From our interviews, two things became evident. First, customers liked it when a salesperson could describe value in economic terms – it helped the customer understand why a solution was priced the way it was and helped the customer communicate the value message to others inside their organization. Second, customers sometimes opted to go with another solution (or no solution at all) even though the economic output of the Value Equation for those other solutions wasn't as compelling. To us, this was a revelation that defied logic. Why would anyone opt for a solution that had a less compelling Value Equation? The more we investigated, the easier it was to understand. This revelation is also the reason we've reassessed the Value Snapshot® tool and have made modifications to make it a more impactful and useful sales tool.

Defying Logic

We have all lost a sale at some point in our career that simply defied logic. We had the best product, we met the client's needs, we had strong relationships, our pricing model was right, etc. When everything seems to be leaning in your favor and a customer still elects to go with a competitor's solution, it can be baffling and frustrating. Our friend, Mike, had just such a situation. Mike had been pursuing an opportunity to position his company's inventory management system with a regional hospital system with five member hospitals. According to Mike, the client was hoping to address issues with inaccurate inventory management and chronic over-ordering. Throughout the sales process, Mike had developed strong relationships with the key influencers, positioned himself well against the competition, and quantified the amount of cost savings his solution could bring compared to the competition. When Mike was told by the customer that they had elected to go with his competition, he was stunned. How could something that felt so right, so quickly go wrong? In our loss analysis interview with this particular client, we learned a few things that surprised even us. First, Mike's Value Equation (Value = Benefits – Cost) was more economically compelling than his competitor. In other words, Mike was able to demonstrate to the key influencers that the benefits he provided outweighed the cost of his solution. Second, there were no mystery adversaries that derailed the deal. Third, the decision criteria described by Mike were nearly identical to the ones described by the customer in the loss analysis. There was one thing that set the competition apart that ultimately tipped the sale in their favor. That one thing was a *Metric.* Sometimes getting the customer to agree that the benefits outweigh the financial commitment isn't enough. In this case, Mike's competitor was able to demonstrate exactly how their solution improved the key business metrics they were striving to impact immediately. Mike's competitor specifically demonstrated how his solution was able to improve inaccurate inventory management and reduce over-ordering. What was more surprising was that Mike's solution was able to accomplish the same outcome, but because Mike's competitor demonstrated exactly *how* his solution would improve those metrics, he was awarded the business.

I Thought We'd Abandoned the Metric System!

In business, nearly everything and everyone – companies, divisions, departments, teams and individuals are all held accountable to something. Goals, Targets, Objectives, Metrics, etc. are all terms used to describe how we measure success. Regardless of the term you use, these measurements exist throughout our customer organizations. When a customer describes a problem they are having, the problem exists because the customer isn't confident they are going to be able to hit that specific goal or metric. For example, a customer might say "We are having issues with employee morale", but the goal or target could be to reduce employee turnover or improve employee satisfaction scores.

In Mike's situation, he knew his customer's problems and showed how his solution could reduce his customer's issues. What Mike didn't do was tie his solution to the metrics (goals, targets, etc.) the customer really cared about. In fact, Mike didn't even know which metrics this customer needed to impact or how those metrics were prioritized. Mike made the natural assumption that economic impact (increasing revenue or decreasing cost) would be a key driver for the customer. Although money is nearly always important, this particular client had other metrics on their mind. There were two key metrics this client wanted to improve. The first was Inventory Turns – the speed in which inventory moves through the system. The second was Chronic Over-Ordering – which meant having systems in place that did automatic ordering when inventory levels fell below a specific threshold. Mike demonstrated to the client how he could help them better manage inventory, but he never tied it back to the metrics that mattered most. The most difficult thing for Mike to swallow was that the connection between his solution and the metrics the client wanted to impact was easy to make, if only he'd helped the client connect the dots.

To Complete the Picture – Connect the Dots

As mentioned earlier, salespeople have been trained for decades to ask questions to uncover and develop customer needs. What they haven't been taught to do is link those needs to customer goals. Some of you might be thinking that this is a minor nuance. However, based on our research, the connection between client needs and client goals is a simple, but essential step that salespeople must learn to make.

When we enter a new sales process with a prospect, we are often told about some common problems or issues they are having. Examples include: "We need to improve our strategic opportunity planning," or "My team doesn't ask enough probing questions in conversations with customers," or "We need help with negotiation skills," These are all statements of needs – and they are excellent starting points for any sales conversations we might have. But these statements do little to clarify how the customer will measure their own success. That is where goals come into play.

Let's use the customer needs statement, "We need help with negotiation skills" as an example. If the customer's sales team had more effective negotiation skills, what key goals might be impacted? Improved margins? Increased top-line revenue? Reduced discounting? Increased revenue from product X that is often given away for free as part of a negotiation? Any of these goals could be impacted if the sales team had better negotiation skills, but which one of these matters most to the customer right now?

A Success Story

Let's see how Susan took the value conversation to another level with one of her key prospects. Susan was approached by a mid-sized, regional based construction company with operations across three states. The executive team was looking for ways to improve the operation of its supply chain network and reduce inventory costs.

When Susan got into her sales process with this client, she did all the right things. She started by getting a handle on the client's needs and expectations, she gained a deep understanding of the client's decision-making process, budget allocation, desired timelines, and identified all of the key stakeholders who would be involved in the process. Susan was even able to use her advocates in the account to gain insight into the competitive landscape.

Susan was up against some formidable competitors, with equally competent solutions and salespeople. She knew that distinguishing herself and her solutions wasn't going to be easy. One of the things that Susan did that immediately distanced herself from the competition in everyone's eyes was to shift the sales conversations she was having with each influencer from needs and wants to objectives and measurements. In her conversations, Susan spent time asking each individual how they were measured and understanding which metrics they hoped to impact by making such an investment.

Just gaining insight into individual and company's goals was something that her competitors weren't doing. What deepened the impact of this was how she linked her solution to those goals and metrics. In our win/loss analysis with this particular client, we spoke with one of the directors of purchasing and heard the following comment: "One of my personal goals was to reduce the number of suppliers by 25 percent. When I first started talking with Susan, I had no idea her solution would help me impact that goal. She not only helped me articulate what I was trying to accomplish, she also demonstrated the impact her solution would have towards that goal. The connection was really helpful for me." We heard these types of comments from multiple influencers inside the account. It didn't matter whether the goal was at a personal or departmental level, Susan's ability to identify the goal, quantify the goal and then demonstrate how her solution impacted the goal was clearly a differentiator.

Converting Needs to Goals

The difference between Susan's and Mike's approach to Value Quantification was subtle. In our win/loss analysis with Mike's opportunities, we found that he could identify problems, quantify those issues and then effectively demonstrate how his solution could address the issue and ultimately save the company money or increase revenue. In nearly every analysis we did for Mike, we found that Mike was able to demonstrate a positive economic story. However, Mike was always linking his value to dollars. Mike seemed to miss really understanding the other business goals or metrics the individuals or departments were striving to improve. In our assessment of Susan's opportunities, we found that she went beyond demonstrating value in monetary terms, and instead broadened the impact of her solution by showing how she could impact a variety of personal, department or corporate goals. Let's face it, as much as we'd like to believe that everyone makes decisions for the good of the company, we know (from our interviews) that people are much more likely to do what's good for them.

Building Your Value Snapshot®

Step #1 – Identify Key Goals

As you suspect, step one in building a Value Snapshot® is to uncover the Goals of the customer. This requires salespeople to implement a skill often overused by four-year-old children – the classic "Why" question. It is essential for salespeople to get beyond simple needs statements and gain a deeper understanding on what the customer is trying to accomplish. In addition to more direct questions, such as "What goals are you trying to impact?" a simple "Why?" can help reveal the client's true purpose in addressing a problem. Keep in mind, goals can exist at multiple levels, i.e. personal, departmental, corporate, etc. It is essential to uncover more than just corporate-level goals so you can begin to understand someone's true motivations and priorities.

Step #2 – Quantify Goals

At some point in your career, you have probably heard the term SMART Goal, which stands for Goals that are Specific, Measurable, Actionable, Realistic, and Time-based. And, while the SMART Goal concept has most of its application in strategic planning, for our purposes, we want to focus on the first two elements of the SMART framework – Specific and Measurable.

Not every goal articulated by a customer is going to be well-defined. Sometimes a goal is ambiguous on purpose, while other times it is a matter of poor planning or lack of consideration. Either way, any goal should be able to be assessed as successful or not regardless of whether a specific metric is tied to it or not. When a customer articulates a goal that is ambiguous in nature, a salesperson should try to determine how the customer is going to measure that goal. When the goal is Specific and Measurable the salesperson will have an easier time demonstrating how their solution can directly impact that goal.

Let's say the reason our customer wants to improve Negotiation Skills is because they believe salespeople are giving away too much top-line revenue. If they want to improve top-line revenue, then what metric are they trying to hit? Do they want to improve top-line revenue by 5 percent, 10 percent, 20 percent, etc.? Is there a specific and measurable number attached to the objective? If not, should there be? If not, can there be? How will the customer measure the success of their investment in Negotiation Skills if they don't know? That is an essential question a salesperson must ask if they are to understand what the customer is really trying to accomplish and if they are to demonstrate measurable value. The answer to this question is not a needs statement – but a goal statement. This shift from needs to goals is a simple, yet powerful way for a salesperson to communicate value. Instead of saying "I can solve your problem," the salesperson can say, "I can help you hit your goal." For some of Mike's losses and Susan's wins, this difference was small enough to shift the balance.

Step #3 – Aligning Your Solution

The third step to build a Value Snapshot®, is to assess how well the customer believes your solution aligns with their goals (or how much of an impact your solution can have on that goal).

This third step is about showing the connection between the customer's goal and the salesperson's solution. This connection could range from a simple understanding of how a solution can affect a goal or to a more robust calculation demonstrating how a solution can have a measured impact on a goal. Regardless, the connection between a solution and a goal must be assessed through the eyes of the customer. The customer needs to recognize and affirm they understand the impact a salesperson's solution can have. It is one thing for the seller to say how their solution can help, it is another thing for the customer to believe it.

Value Snapshot® – What does the Picture Tell You?

It is always nice to know whether there is enough value in your solution to provide sound justification to the customer *before* they make their final decision. By knowing the value position ahead of time, an effective salesperson will have time to do something about it. When completed, the Value Snapshot®, like the other Snapshot tools, provides a visual image of your situation. The Value Snapshot® provides a visual image of the potential value you bring to the opportunity by highlighting the Quantified Goals of the customer and how well the customer believes your solutions align to those goals.

Below is a Value Snapshot® that was completed by Susan for the opportunity described earlier in the chapter. This Snapshot was completed in the early stages of the opportunity while there was still time for her to impact the situation.

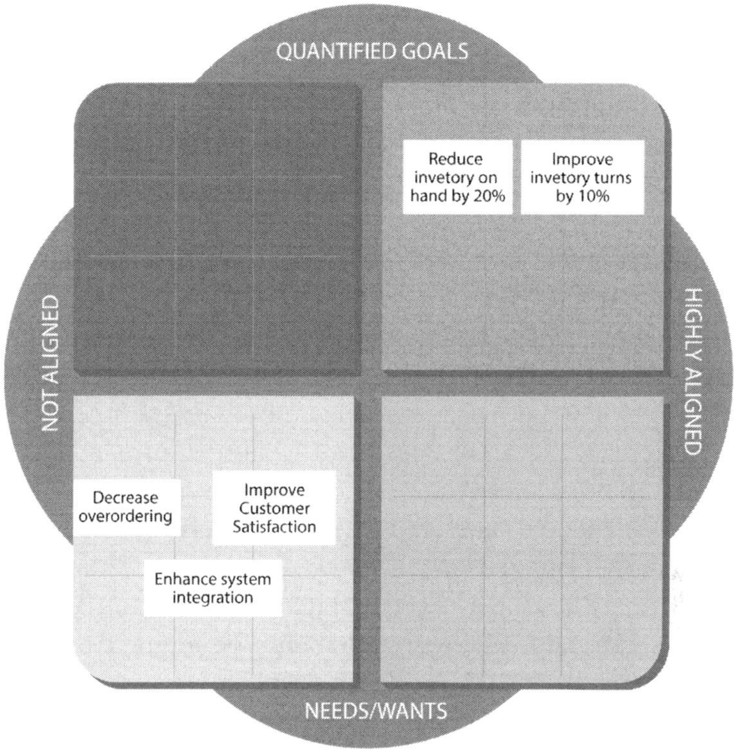

When looking at this picture, Susan asked herself the following three questions:

1. ***What's missing?*** A primary aim for any salesperson selling in a complex situation is to ensure they have a complete and full understanding of the customer's goals and issues. Susan had spent considerable time discussing needs and issues with the customer and had gained a solid understanding of the problems the customer was hoping to address with the new inventory management system. However, when Susan had her initial conversations with the customer, she was only told about their aim to improve inventory turns and reduce the amount of inventory on hand.

   Susan knew that her solution's unique ability to integrate with the customer's other system, including the company's CRM system, needed to be put into the mind of the customer. By asking questions about what might happen if the customer's sales force continued to lack insight into the company's inventory levels, Susan got the customer to acknowledge two things; first there were problems with salespeople submitting orders outside of the current inventory management system for products that were already in stock, causing unnecessary over-ordering; and second, making promises to customers about products that were already out of stock and hard to get. The customer had not initially given adequate consideration to the need for enhanced systems integration or make the connection between the inventory management system and improved customer satisfaction.

2. ***What goals will be impacted if these problems are solved?*** The elements on Susan's initial Value Snapshot® are all statements of problems and needs, none of which are linked to specific and measurable goals. However, with a little work and a few questions, you can link each problem to key metrics and demonstrate how the solution can impact those metrics. The easy ones are Inventory Turns and Inventory on Hand. These are already metrics that can be assessed by evaluating the company's balance sheet and inventory levels. Tougher ones to assess are Enhanced Integration with other Systems and Improved Customer Satisfaction. These are definitely statements of "want," but what metrics or goals can each of these statements be aligned to? That was the challenge for Susan. What Susan found when she asked the question, "How do you measure Customer Satisfaction?" and "What goals do you have for Customer Satisfaction metrics?" was that her primary point of contact (in the case the CIO and Director of Operations) didn't have the answers. Just by asking these questions, Susan gained access to new influencers who could be impacted positively by her solution. This ultimately led Susan to improve not only the Value Snapshot®, but the Influencer Snapshot® as well by adding additional advocates for her solution.

3. ***What specific impact can my solution have on your goals?*** With a more solid understanding of the customers' problems and the goals that would be impacted if those problems were addressed, it was important for Susan to demonstrate how well-aligned her solutions were to those goals. Let's say the customer wanted to reduce the amount of inventory on hand by 10 percent. Could Susan's solution help them accomplish that goal completely or just partially? Susan had to work to get the customer to recognize not only how her solutions could help, but also by how much. Susan not only needed to present her solutions in a very specific way, but also get the customer to quantify the impact her solutions could have toward the goals they were trying to accomplish.

After assessing these three areas and getting the customer to commit to the value of her solution, Susan's Value Snapshot® looked very different. It also looked like a winning picture – and it was.

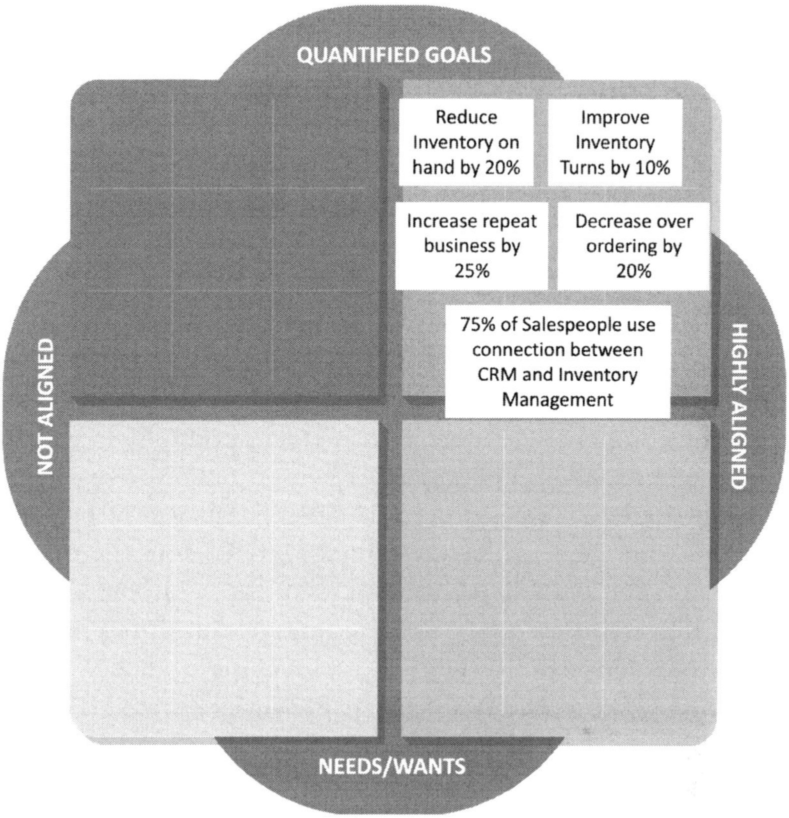

Susan developed a winning Value Snapshot®. Unfortunately, building a winning Value Snapshot® takes strategy and execution. When working with the Value Snapshot®, there are three common issues and ways to address them:

1. **Too Few Goals** – Although It doesn't happen very often, there are some sales situations where we find the customer doesn't have any specific or measurable reasons behind making a purchase. There are no problems or goals the customer is trying to address, at least not on the surface. A customer could consider a purchase because they have budget they need to spend, or because they have an existing solution that is no longer working or because it is simply time to make a change. People buy things all the time because they want them, but not because it is addressing some significant goal they need to achieve.

In our space, for example we've had customers approach us about buying a sales training solution for no other apparent reason than to create a "common sales language." Many salespeople would be satisfied with this statement and would present a solution for one common sales training solution across the organization. But, how do you measure the value of that? If customers don't fully understand what goals or metrics can be impacted by such an investment, then the salesperson must take the responsibility to educate the customer and help them see the connection between the investment and the things they need to impact.

Our solutions have the potential to create value for customers even when no needs or goals are apparent. But this takes work. It also takes skill. Susan knew that her software solution had a unique attribute. For one, her inventory management software had the ability to integrate with her customer's CRM system, thus providing her customer's sales teams the ability to look at their company's existing inventory levels. Nearly all of Susan's customers appreciated this integration component and believed it was important. However, if Susan asked a question, such as, "What goal of yours would be most impacted by this unique attribute?" the customer was clueless. Instead of positioning her solution in this manner and getting dumbfounded looks from customers, Susan took a different tact. In addition to asking the customers to share their goals and objectives, Susan considered her unique capabilities and challenged the customer to consider life without them. Questions such as, "If your salespeople don't have visibility into your inventory system, what happens?" or "If salespeople tell a customer a product is available and it's not, what's the impact?" As Susan continues to engage the customer in this dialogue, she learns about problems that exist today (with the existing solution) and problems that could exist in the absence of her unique capabilities. As we already learned, it isn't difficult to make a connection between a need and a goal. However, in the absence of a need, you have to create one.

2. **Missing Metrics** – The y-axis on the Value Snapshot® assesses whether statements made by the customer are simply acknowledgement of a problem or confirmation of the quantified goals the customer needs to impact. As you begin to compile a list of customer's goals, the Value Snapshot® begins to take shape. It isn't uncommon for conversations with customers early in the sales cycle to be focused on problems and needs. However, as the salesperson deepens his/her understanding of what the customer is trying to accomplish, the goals and objectives should become more specific and quantifiable. If you look at the Value Snapshot® and see that most of the customer statements are not linked

to goals, or are not quantified, then you have some missing metrics you need to uncover or quantify.

3. **Lack of Connection** – A salesperson's job is all about showing how his/her products and services align to customer needs and goals. Sometimes the connection is obvious, while other times the salesperson has to work diligently to connect the dots for the customer. The x-axis on the Value Snapshot® is used to assess how closely the customer believes the salesperson's solution aligns with the customer's goals. When completing the Value Snapshot®, it is essential that the salesperson assess how well the *customer* believes the salesperson's solutions align with the customer's goals. Too many salespeople make the mistake of assessing the connection from their own perspective and make the assumption the customer sees the link.

Chapter 6 Summary

In this chapter, we covered how you can better align your solutions to the quantifiable goals of your customer.

This involves three steps:

1. Identify the goals your customer is striving to improve. Remember, you're likely to discover that there are Corporate Goals, Divisional/Department Goals and Personal/Individual Goals. The better you can articulate those goals from each level, the greater your chances are to win.

2. Quantify the goals your customer has shared with you. Simply knowing your customer wants to increase margins is good, but knowing they want to increase margins by six percent in the next 12 months is even better.

3. The final step is to effectively align how your solution, specifically your unique capabilities, directly impacts the quantifiable goals your customer is striving to achieve. Getting your customer to quantify the specific impact your solution will have on their goal is definitely going to improve the likelihood of you winning.

Being able to execute these three simple steps can make the difference between you winning or losing an opportunity. Our research shows that one out of three salespeople will invest the time to explore a need stated by the customer and ask the questions necessary to get the customer to state a quantifiable goal. As we've demonstrated in our win/loss analysis, those salespeople that make a little extra effort to understand their customers' quantifiable goals are more likely to win.

Chapter Questions

These questions are designed to engage you in understanding how to better identify the quantifiable goals of your customer and effectively align your solutions to those goals. Like in the previous chapters, think of a current sales opportunity you are working on, and ask yourself these questions:

1. What are the top three or four goals your customer is striving to improve in the next 12 months that your solution can directly impact?

2. Which of those goals are currently quantifiable and which are not? What questions should you ask to get the customer to turn the non-quantifiable goals into quantifiable goals?

3. Determine how well your solution is aligned to the customers' goals by asking what unique capabilities your solution offers that can directly align to help the customer achieve their goals?

4. When assessing those goals to which your solutions are directly aligned, what question can you ask to get the customer to state the potential quantifiable impact your solution may potentially have on their goal?

CHAPTER 7

Summary Chapter

The Strategic Snapshot Tools and Challenge Questions we provided in this book are designed to help you win more and lose less. Our hope is that these tools help you do four things differently; Slow down. Think Critically. Challenge your Assumptions. Execute Strategically.

Let's reiterate the first two sentences you read in Chapter 1:

"This book is a project we originally conceived as a way to codify and disseminate many of the client assessments, win/loss analyses and best practices we've observed over the years. It is our hope that it helps salespeople better analyze opportunities and develop strategic opportunity plans to help accelerate your pipeline revenue, beat out the competition and win more business."

When used appropriately, the process and strategic opportunity-planning

Snapshot tools we provide in this book can minimize the need for lost opportunity post-mortems by helping you win more and lose less.

The purpose of this chapter is to give you a quick overview of what we've covered in the previous chapters. Refer back to it to refresh the key points of each chapter in a hurry.

Chapter 1 Summary: Strategizing for Success

In Chapter 1, we introduced you to our two main characters, Susan and Mike. You showed how these two salespeople, Susan—a top performer, and Mike—an average performer, have different approaches to the strategic management of key sales opportunities.

With Susan, you saw an individual who approached the management of opportunities with more discipline, closely following the six-stage sales pipeline process her company had developed and minimizing the number of assumptions she made about influencers, competitors, process, etc. Susan was disciplined in her use of strategy tools. She used those tools to paint a clear picture of the opportunity and to develop effective strategies to improve her position.

Mike, on the other hand, took a more casual approach to opportunity management. He frequently skipped critical milestones in his company's well-defined sales process and made the critical mistake of making too many assumptions about his current situation, based on past experience. Make no mistake – Mike still won a lot of sales opportunities, but he also lost his fair share.

The goal of this first chapter was to set the stage for Susan and Mike, and to show you how each of them approached the strategic planning components described in following chapters. When the great Michael Jordan joined the NBA and signed his shoe and apparel contract with Nike, the ad slogan "Be Like Mike" became widely known. In our book, we don't want you to "Be Like Mike". We want you to "Be Like Susan". It may not have the same ring to it, but it is the lesson we want to teach!

Chapter 2 Summary: Constructing Your Sales Pipeline

In Chapter 2, we shared what it takes to build your pipeline. A "well-defined sales pipeline" is like a salesperson's "recipe for success." If it is built right, the sales pipeline will consist of clearly defined steps – what we call **critical milestones**. We defined a critical milestone as a strategic action that if not taken, could put the opportunity at risk.

Now that you have the proper tools and resources to start building your pipeline, ask yourself: "How can I build my pipeline to where I can succeed in winning every opportunity throughout each carefully curated step in the process?"

Rome wasn't built in a day, nor was its plumbing when that infrastructure came about. Choosing which experts in your company should be a part of your new sales pipeline design will soon prove to be an asset, helping you identify the stages and critical milestones that define your sales pipeline process.

Have you ever heard that a worker is only as good as their tools? Once you've gathered the top performers in your company and identified your critical milestones, you have to provide your team with the right tools and resources to help effectively execute and achieve those milestones.

Chapter 3 Summary: Situational Snapshot®

In Chapter 3, we introduced you to a tool called the Situational Snapshot®, which provides a visual depiction of strategic position for an opportunity based on five critical buying factors. These five critical buying factors below exist for every sales opportunity:

- Knowing the length of the customer decision process.
- Determining the level of complexity in the decision process and what's driving it.
- Finding, or creating, a sense of urgency within the customer.
- Identifying if there's a consensus between the key influencer(s) around

the buying decision.
- Knowing your competitive position based upon who your competition is.

Once you have a complete and accurate understanding of the five buying factors for the, the salesperson can populate the Situational Snapshot® tool. Utilizing the Situational Snapshot® will help you assess your strategic position for an opportunity, determine the strengths and weaknesses of each buying factor, recognize the relationship between the buying factors and analyze how shifts in any factor can impact the overall situation and, thus, the sale outcome.

Situational Snapshot®

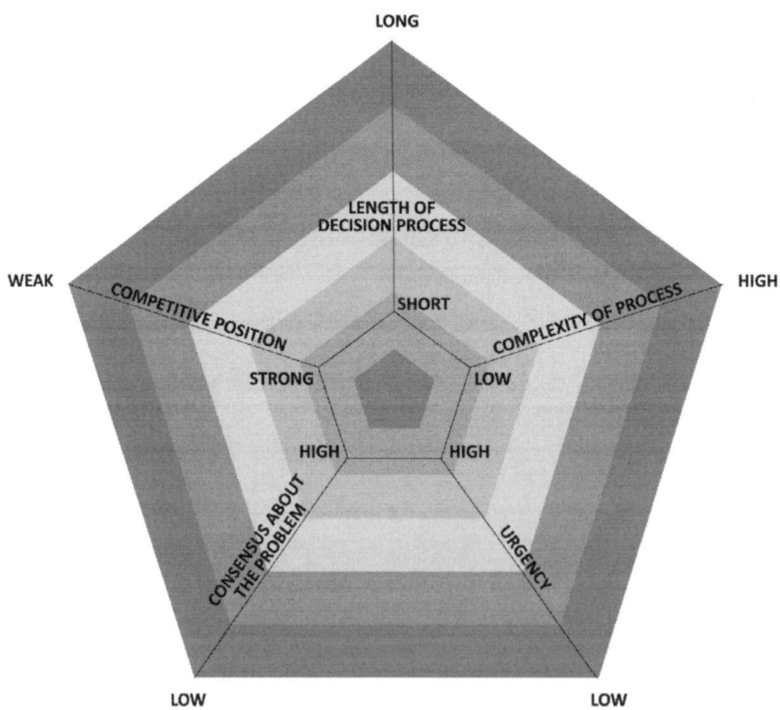

Chapter 4 Summary: Influencer Snapshot®

Research supports the idea that companies are becoming more conscientious about assessing the economic impact of purchases, more regimented in their evaluation of competitive alternatives and, lastly, the ways in which companies are engaging more Key Influencers in the decision-making process through the use of decision or value analysis committees.

Identifying and managing the Key Influencers engaged with your opportunity is vital to the success of your sales strategy. In addition, knowing how to leverage your Advocates and minimize the impact of your Adversaries is crucial for overarching success. Using Ignite Selling's Influencer Snapshot® tool and the steps discussed in Chapter 4, you will have the right tools to determine who your Key Influencers are, understand the amount of influence they exert in the decision-making process, and determine the best approach to leverage your Advocates and minimize the impact of your Adversaries.

To build and accurate and complete Influencer Snapshot®, follow the three steps described below:

- Identify *all* of the key players who may exert influence in the decision-making process.
- Determine how each key influencer feels about you– are they an advocate or an adversary?
- Gauge the relative level of influence each key influencer has in the buying process.

With a clear and accurate Influencer Snapshot®, you can determine the appropriate movement strategies (#1 - To the Right→ by changing the way that person perceives you, making them less adversarial to your cause; #2 - Down→ by reducing that person's level of influence in the decision-making process; #3 - Down and to the Right→ a combination of #1 and #2) needed to improve your chances of winning. Let's face it, getting all of the key influencers to become advocates is an unlikely aim in many situations. However, a well-executed sales strategy can succeed even when there are adversaries working against you.

Influencer Snapshot®

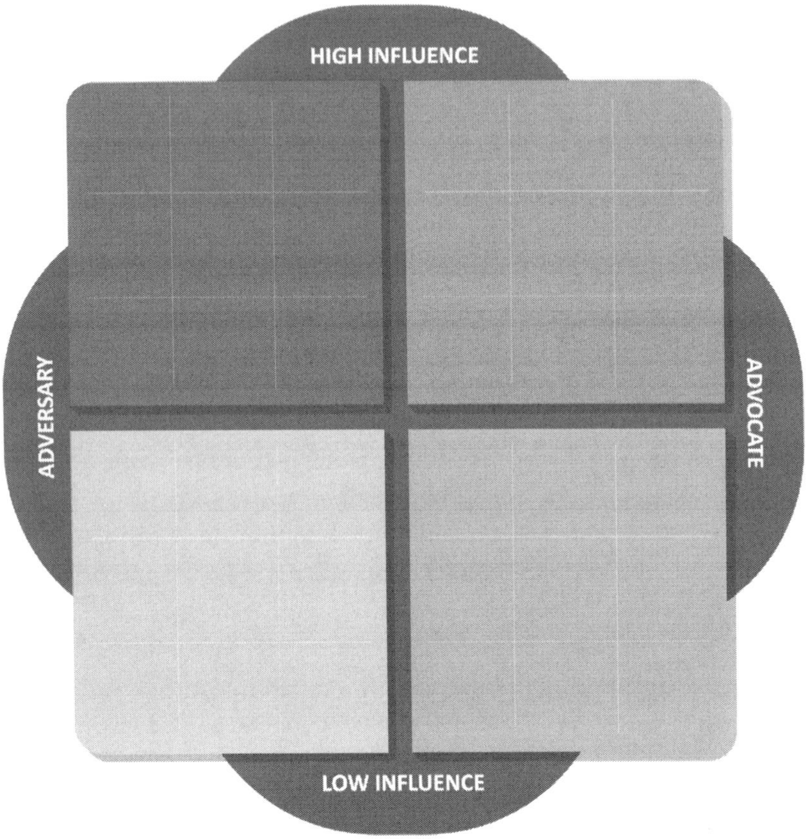

Chapter 5 Summary: Competitive Snapshot®

In our research, 86 percent of salespeople surveyed believe that price was the number-one reason they lost their last sale. However, after conducting a loss analysis and speaking to many of those customers that opted to work with another supplier, we heard a different story. In those interviews, only 19 percent of those surveyed said they made a decision based on price. It seems that salespeople are NOT losing to "price" as often as they believe. So, if price isn't the culprit for a lost sale, what is?

In Chapter 5, introduced a tool called the Competitive Snapshot®. The Competitive Snapshot® is a visual tool that provides a strategic overview of a seller's competitive position for a given opportunity. When customers make decisions between competing alternatives, they use Decision Criteria as a way of comparing one solution to another. The Competitive Snapshot® provides an overview of the customer's perspective on those decision criteria, depicting what's important to the customer and how they believe our solutions match up against the competition.

The following four steps are required to build a complete and accurate Competitive Snapshot®:

- Identify the decision criteria your customer is using to compare you against the competition.
- Add additional decision criteria you believe the customer has not considered. (Typically, those items that differentiate you from your competitors.)
- Determine how the customer ranks the decision criteria from Most Essential to Least Essential.
- Confirm with your customer whether they perceive your ability to meet their decision criteria as Comparatively Good or Comparatively Bad when weighed against the competition.

Once you have a clear picture of the competitive landscape through the Competitive Snapshot®, you can develop movement strategies to reinforce or enhance the need to meet those decision criteria where you are comparatively good, and effectively manage the decision criteria where you are comparatively bad.

Competitive Snapshot®

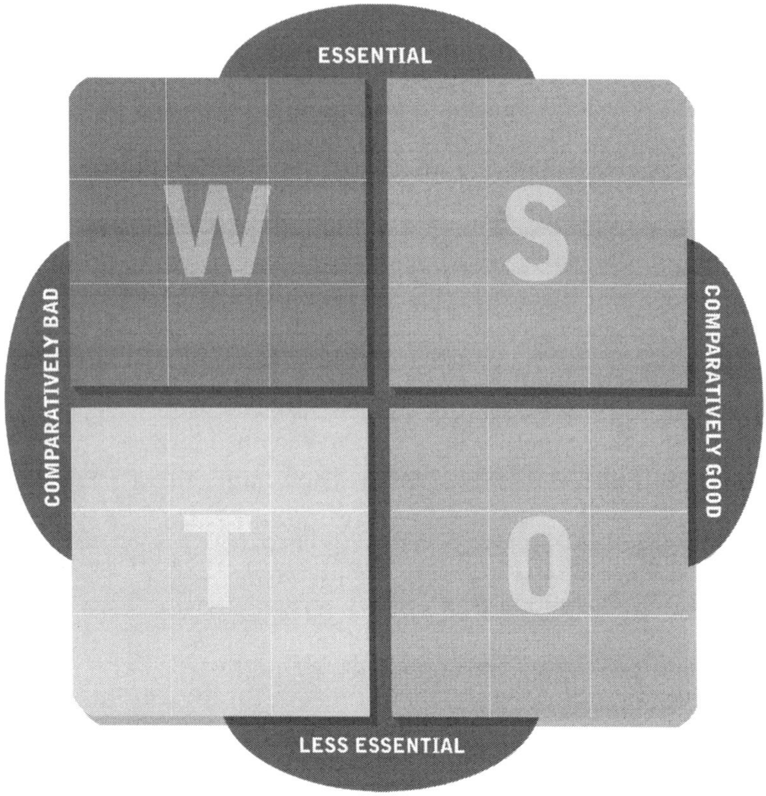

Chapter 6 Summary: Value Snapshot®

Assessing Value is not as easy as it sounds. For years, salespeople have been told to uncover, develop and quantify the needs of their customers. The idea that the value of a solution goes hand in hand with problem solving is very compelling. Even more compelling is the idea that you quantify the value in monetary terms by calculating the impact a solution can have on top-line revenue growth (i.e. growing sales) or in cost reduction efforts (i.e. efficiency improvements). Unfortunately, not everyone is held accountable to economic measurements. However, everyone (and every department, every division, etc.) is held accountable to something. Everyone has goals they are trying to achieve – metrics they are trying to impact - or targets they are trying to hit. It's often how people are measured on the job.

While demonstrating economic value has proven to be effective, especially for premium priced solutions, what research has shown has more impact on a buyer's decision-making selection process is a direct correlation between the solutions they are considering and the goals they are trying to attain. To succeed, salespeople need to have a deeper understanding of the business metrics that matter most to the customer they are speaking to. Salespeople need to know what their customers are being held accountable to and demonstrate the quantifiable impact the solution can have on that goal.

The Value Snapshot® is a visual depiction of the Value the salesperson can bring to the customer by demonstrating quantifiable impact on the customer's goals and critical metrics. To build a complete and accurate Value Snapshot®, a salesperson needs to complete the following steps:

- Identify the needs of the customer.
- Determine what personal, departmental, company goals are impacted if the needs are not met.
- Quantify how those goals are assessed and success is measured.
- Assess how much of an impact the Customer believes the sellers solution will have on that goal.

A complete and accurate Value Snapshot® gives the salesperson a sound perspective on the perceived value their solution is bringing the customer. Understanding how the customer perceives the value empowers the salesperson to develop and implement strategies to change the value equation by strengthening the connection between solutions and metrics, or by enhancing the specificity of the metrics the customer is using to measure success.

Value Snapshot®

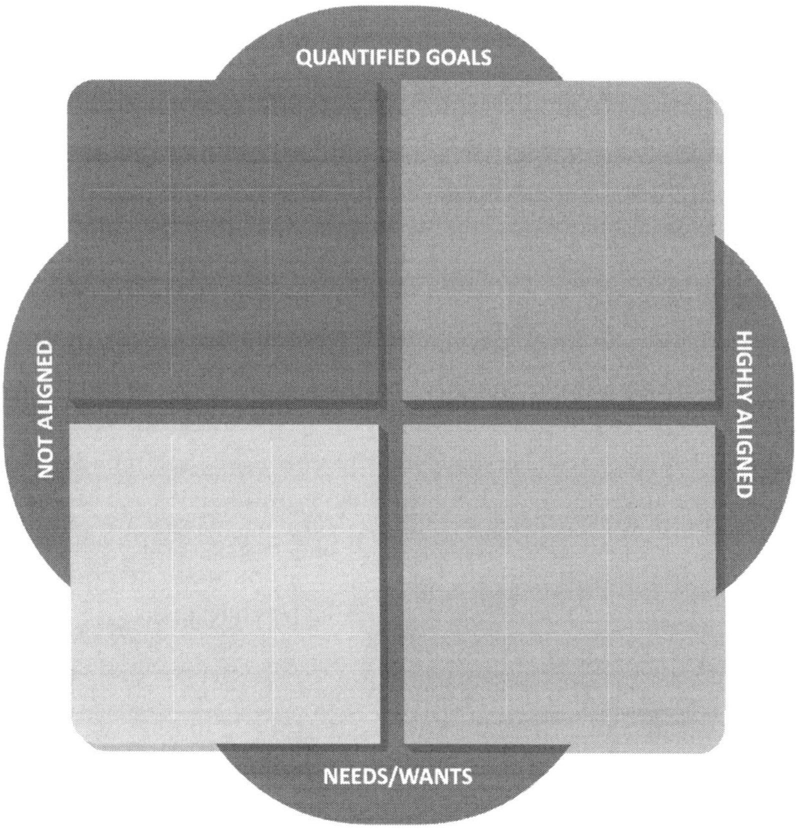

Now, Go Ignite *Your* Sales Strategies

After reading this book, you should now be aware of the tools and resources available to develop your sales strategy for every unique opportunity in each of your accounts. You're encouraged to challenge the assumptive mindset that often comes along with closing high-value and high-pressure sales opportunities.

When used appropriately, the process and strategic opportunity-planning Snapshot tools provided in this book will minimize the need for lost opportunity post-mortems by helping you win more and lose less– after all, that's the essence of selling, is it not?

Earlier, at the beginning of this Summary Chapter, we reminded you of the first two sentences you read in Chapter 1. We would like to leave you now with another key takeaway from Chapter 1:

"As sales leaders ourselves, we know how books like this get used. Some folks embrace these ideas in whole or in part and begin implementing them straight away. Ironically, this book is not really meant for them; they are top performers because they are already doing much of what we describe. Other salespeople may read this book but choose to disregard the ideas completely, despite the fact that those are the people who typically have the most to gain from implementing these 'success ideas.'

"However, it is neither the top performer nor the low performer who we had in mind when we conceived this book. It's the lot in the middle we wrote it for, the salespeople who hit their numbers but still have room to grow. They win some and lose some, like most salespeople, but they ought to be winning more than they are losing."

It is true that we conceived this book with neither the top performer nor the low performer in mind– it is, in fact, the average performer who we wrote it for; and it will, in fact, always remain true that those salespeople who fall somewhere in the middle should win more than they lose.

So, we have one final question for you before you start implementing strategic opportunity plans and accelerating your pipeline revenue: Are you going to lose your next sale? Or are you going to use the tools provided in this field guide and invest time in the right accounts, develop your strategic thinking and, ultimately, begin to win more business by successfully following up on the right opportunities?

The choice is yours.

About the Authors

Steve Gielda

For more than 25 years, Steve has been helping companies throughout the world improve their sales performance, accelerate their sales revenues and meet their business goals. Steve is a salesperson to the core—he loves working with clients, understanding their needs and helping them improve their business outcomes.

Steve started his career at Lanier Worldwide, pounding the pavement and knocking on doors. His success as a salesperson and his desire to take on leadership roles allowed Steve to move into the positions of District Manager and Region Sales Director. Steve's success comes from his persistence and willingness to forge strong client relationships.

He understands the importance of building smart sales strategies that are linked to driving his clients' business goals. Steve began his career in sales enablement in 1997 when he joined Huthwaite, Inc. Steve later established his own practice as a partner with the Advantage Performance Group, then later as a principal with Sales Momentum.

In 2010, Steve and Kevin joined together to form Ignite Selling, Inc.

Kevin Jones

For more than 25 years, Kevin has been designing and delivering training solutions that impact people's lives. Kevin's goal is to create a learning environment where participants can thrive and where lessons learned can be translated to the field. Kevin has worked in finance, sales and sales training. It was in sales training that Kevin found his true passion—developing people.

Kevin received a bachelor's degree in business from North Carolina State University and a master's in business administration from the Kenan-Flagler Business School at the University of North Carolina at Chapel Hill. Kevin uses his academic exposure and real-world experience to develop training solutions that drive business results. Kevin's work has enabled him to influence hundreds of companies in more than 30 countries worldwide.

In 2010, Steve and Kevin joined together to form Ignite Selling, Inc.